EARLY SETTLERS

OF

NANTUCKET

THEIR ASSOCIATES AND
DESCENDANTS

COMPILED BY

LYDIA S. HINCHMAN

JANAWAY PUBLISHING
Santa Maria, California

<u>Notice</u>

In many older books, foxing (or discoloration) occurs and, in some instances, print lightens with wear and age. Reprinted books, such as this, often duplicate these flaws, notwithstanding efforts to reduce or eliminate them. The pages of this reprint have been digitally enhanced and, where possible, the flaws eliminated in order to provide clarity of content and a pleasant reading experience.

CONTENTS.

PAGE

DEEDS OF PURCHASE AND SETTLEMENT OF THE ISLAND—Discovery—Names of Purchasers—Ten Proprietors added—Houses built—Town named 7

THOMAS MACY—Arrival in America—His Record in Salisbury, Massachusetts—Violation of Laws in Religious Matters—Admonition—Apology—Departure for Nantucket 17

EDWARD STARBUCK—Settlement at Dover, New Hampshire—Possessions in Dover—Profession of Anabaptism—Joins Thomas Macy on his Voyage to Nantucket—Name of Starbuck associated with his Former Possessions until 1716 21

TRISTRAM COFFIN—Birth—Marriage—Arrival in America—Early Ancestry—Coffin Home in Normandy and England—Life and Services at Nantucket—Commission as Chief Magistrate of Colony—Sketch of his Children 24

ADMIRAL SIR ISAAC COFFIN—His Early Life in Boston—. Interest in Nantucket—Services for the King—Marriage and Death in England 33

CHRISTOPHER HUSSEY—Marriage—Arrival in Boston—Settlement at Hampton, New Hampshire—Public Services—STEPHEN HUSSEY 37

STEPHEN GREENLEAF, WITH SOME ACCOUNT OF HIS FATHER, EDMUND GREENLEAF—Origin of the Family—Arrival in America of Edmund Greenleaf and Family—Public Service—Extract from Will—STEPHEN GREENLEAF as Proprietor of Nantucket—Military Life—Death 40

PAGE

JOHN GREENLEAF WHITTIER—Detail of Descent from Tristram Coffin and Stephen Greenleaf   43

OTHER PROPRIETORS—ROBERT PIKE—Settlement at Salisbury—Relations with Nantucket—Public Life—THOMAS COLEMAN as Proprietor—THOMAS AND ROBERT BARNARD—Proprietors of Nantucket—Thomas Barnard's Return to England—Robert Barnard's Family—Ezra Cornell—RICHARD SWAIN—Connection of his Family with Weare Family, of Hampton, New Hampshire—JOHN SWAIN as Proprietor—His House   44

PETER FOLGER—Origin of Folger Family—Peter Folger's Arrival in America—Life and Missionary Work at Martha's Vineyard—Cotton Mather's Description of Him—Settlement at Nantucket—His Family—Benjamin Franklin and his Descendants in Philadelphia—Walter Folger—Maria Mitchell—Jacob Barker—Thomas Prence—William Collier—William Allen Butler—Charles James Folger . .   47

THOMAS, JOHN, AND RICHARD GARDINER—Settlement in America—Life at Cape Ann and Salem—Removal of RICHARD GARDNER to Nantucket—Richard as Magistrate—JOHN GARDNER as Magistrate on Nantucket, Judge of Probate, and Captain of " Ffoot Company "   55

SAMUEL SHATTUCK—Association of Name with Nantucket—Persecution—Banishment from America—Samuel Shattuck's Return to America with the King's Mandate   60

THOMAS MAYHEW AND THOMAS MAYHEW, JR.—Thomas Mayhew as Proprietor of Nantucket—His Life at Martha's Vineyard—Missionary Work of Thomas Mayhew, Jr., among Indians—Children and Descendants of Thomas Mayhew, Jr.   68

EXTRACTS FROM JOURNALS OF JOHN RICHARDSON AND THOMAS STORY, GIVING SOME ACCOUNT OF THE RISE OF FRIENDS ON NANTUCKET—Establishment of Friends' Meeting—Present Condition of the Society on the Island   72

PAGE

AN IMPARTIAL JUDGMENT 80

DETAIL OF DESCENT FROM PROPRIETORS AND SETTLERS:

    Mitchell Family 83
    Russell Family 85
    Barker Family 90
    Swain Family 93
    Family of Lucretia Mott 94
    Families of Thomas Earle and John Milton Earle 98
    Swift Family 100
    Rotch Family 104
    Bunker Family 107
    Wing and Hathaway Connection with Nantucket 110
    Coggeshall Connection with Nantucket 112
    Buffum Connection with Nantucket 114
    Stanton Connection with Nantucket 116

APPENDIX 119

EARLY SETTLERS OF NANTUCKET.

DEEDS OF PURCHASE AND SETTLEMENT OF THE ISLAND.

BELKNAP, in his Biography of Biron,* says, "An Icelander of the name Herioff and his son Biron * made a voyage every year to different countries for the sake of traffic.

"About the beginning of the eleventh century (1001) their ships were separated by a storm. When Biron * arrived in Norway he heard that his father was gone to Greenland, and he resolved to follow him; but another storm drove him to the southwest, where he discovered a flat country, free from rocks, but covered with thick woods, and an island near the coast."

When on his return to Greenland his discoveries became known, Lief, the son of Eric, Earl of Norway, equipped a vessel, and "taking Biron* for his pilot sailed (1002) in search of the new country."

Belknap says, "Biarne's * description of the coast is very accurate and in the island situate to the eastward (between which and the promontory that stretches to the eastward and northward Lief sailed) we recognize Nantucket. The Ancient Northmen found there many

---

* Bjorne.

7

shallows." There is little doubt that Nantucket was visited by Englishmen very early in the seventeenth century (1602).

In the biography of Gosnold, Belknap says, "The shoal water and breach which he calls Tucker's Terror corresponds with the shoal and breakers called Pollock's Rip. . . . To avoid this danger it being late in the day he stood so far out to sea as to overshoot the eastern entrance of what is now called the Vineyard Sound.

"The land which he made in the night was a white cliff on the eastern coast of Nantucket now called Sankoty Head.

"The breach which lay off Gilbert's Point I take to be the Bass Rip and the Pollock Rip with the cross ripplings which extend from the southeast extremity of that island.

"Over these ripplings there is a depth of water from four to seven fathoms, according to a late map of Nantucket, published by Peleg Coffin, Esq., and others." *

It is difficult to imagine any native of Nantucket who would not be interested in facts relating to its history, whether geographical, historical, geological, or genealogical; but the practical interest for us of the present day dates from 1659, when it was finally settled by sturdy men, ancestors to so many in this broad land that a brief detail of the public services of those pioneers cannot fail to be of value to their descendants.

Tradition assigns two causes for the sudden departure

---

* American Biography. By Jeremy Belknap, D.D. With Additions and Notes by F. M. Hubbard. Published by Harper & Brothers in 1848.

of Thomas Macy and Edward Starbuck from Salisbury, Massachusetts.

Many of their descendants have believed that persecution on account of the harboring of Quakers led those early settlers to leave an already established home, to seek another upon a desolate, bleak island, where skulking Indians, added to its isolated position, made a most inhospitable landing-place.

On the other hand, most historians attribute the journey of Thomas Macy and Edward Starbuck in 1659 to a business negotiation pending between them and Thomas Mayhew in regard to the purchase of the island of Nantucket.

Benjamin Franklin Folger, one of the well-known genealogists of Nantucket, has stated that early in 1659 Tristram Coffin went on a voyage of investigation, first to Martha's Vineyard, where he secured the services of Peter Folger as interpreter, thence to Nantucket, "his object being to ascertain the temper and disposition of the Indians and the capabilities of the island that he might report to the citizens of Salisbury what inducements for emigration thither were offered."

Thomas Mayhew, some years before, had received a grant of the islands off the southeast coast of Massachusetts from William, Earl of Sterling, and Sir Fernando or Ferdinand Gorges, as is shown by the records

---

Note.—In 1641 Nantucket appears to have been under the control of William, Earl of Sterling, and Sir Fernando or Ferdinand Gorges, as "during this year the Elizabeth Islands, Caparrock or Martha's Vineyard, Nanticon or Nantucket and Tuckanuck or Tuckanuckett" were "graunted unto Thomas Mayhew at Watertowne, Merchant, and to Thomas Mayhew his sonne."

The consideration named in the deed of Nantucket was "that Thomas Mayhew and Thomas Mayhew his sonne or either of them or their Assignes doe render and pay yearly unto the Honᵇˡᵉ the Lord

in the secretary's office at Albany, New York, Nantucket having belonged to New York until about 1690.

In 1659 the island or the patent of it was still in the possession of the Mayhews.

F. B. Hough's book says, "In 1659 the elder Mayhew admitted nine others to a joint partnership in the Island of Nantucket, reserving a small part to himself, and in February following it was agreed that each Partner might admit another to an equal share in Power and Interest, not being justly excepted to by the Rest."

We find on record that in July of 1659 a deed was given by Thomas Mayhew, confirming the sale of the island of Nantucket to nine purchasers,—viz. :

TRISTRAM COFFIN.
RICHARD SWAIN, or SWAYNE.
PETER COFFIN.
STEPHEN GREENLEAF.
WILLIAM PIKE.
THOMAS MACY.
THOMAS BARNARD.
CHRISTOPHER HUSSEY.
JOHN SWAIN, or SWAYNE.

Copy of Deed of Nantucket to Nine Purchasers (dated July 2, 1659).

"Recorded for Mr Coffin and Mr Macy afores⁴ ye Day and Year afores⁴.

Sterling, his Heyres and Assignes, such an acknowledgement as shall be thought fitt by John Winthrop Esqʳ the Elder or any two Magistrates in the Massachusetts Bay, being Chosen for that End and Purpose by the Honᵇˡᵉ the Lord Sterling or his Deputy and by the said Thomas Mayhew and Thomas Mayhew his Sonne, or their Assignes." This deed was dated October 18, 1641.

" Be it known unto all Men by these Presents that I,
Thomas Mayhew of Martha's Vineyard, Merchant,
doe hereby acknowledge that I have sould unto Tristram Coffin, Thomas Macy, Christopher Hussey, Richard Swayne, Thomas Bernard, Peter Coffin, Stephen
Greenleafe, John Swayne and William Pike that Right
and Interest I have in ye Land of Nantuckett by Patent;
y⁰ wᶜʰ Right I bought of James Fforrett, Gent. and
Steward to y⁰ Lord Sterling and of Richard Vines,
sometimes of Sacho, Gent., Steward-Genʳˡˡ unto Sir
Georges Knight as by Conveyances under their Hands
and Seales doe appeare, ffor them y⁰ aforesaid to Injoy,
and their Heyres and Assignes forever wᵗʰ all the
Privileges thereunto belonging, for in consideration of
y⁰ Sume of Thirty Pounds of Current Pay unto whomsoever I y⁰ said Thomas Mayhew, mine Heyres or Assignes shall appoint.

" And also two Beaver Hatts one for myself and one
for my wife.

" And further this is to declare that I the said
Thomas Mayhew have received to myself that Neck
upon Nantucket called Masquetuck or that Neck of
Land called Nashayte the Neck (but one) northerly of
Masquetuck, y⁰ aforesaid Sayle in anywise notwithstanding. And further, I y⁰ said Thomas Mayhew am
to beare my Part of the Charge of y⁰ said Purchase
above named, and to hold one twentieth Part of all
Lands purchased already, or shall be hereafter purchased, upon y⁰ said Island by y⁰ aforesᵈ Purchasʳˢ or
Heyres and Assignes forever.

" Briefly: It is thus: That I really sold all my Patent
to y⁰ aforesaid nine Men and they are to pay mee or
whomsoever I shall appoint them, y⁰ sume of Thirty
Pounds in good Marchantable Pay in y⁰ Massachu-

setts, under wch Governm^t they now Inhabit, and 2
Beaver Hatts, and I am to beare a 20th Part of y^e
Charge of ye Purchase, and to have a 20th Part of all
Lands and Priviledges; and to have wch of ye Necks
afors^d that I will myselfe, paying for it; only ye Purchasers are to pay what ye Sachem is to have for Masquetuck, although I have ye other Neck.

"And in witness hereof I have hereunto sett my
Hand and Seale this second Day of July sixteen hundred and fifty-nine—(1659).

"Per me

"Tho. Mayhew.

"Witness   John Smith
     "Edward Searle."

By this deed it will be observed that a share of the
island was retained by Thomas Mayhew, and in this
way he became one of the proprietors who are said in
all histories of the place to have founded the settlement.

The following deed proves that notwithstanding the
purchase of the island from Thomas Mayhew, a business negotiation was made with the Indians also, and
that the land was fairly bought from them:

DEED OF WANACKMANACK.

"This witnesseth that I, Wanackmanack, Chief
Sachem of Nantucket hath sold unto Mr. Tristram
Coffin and Thomas Macy their heirs and assigns that
whole neck of land called by the Indians Pacummoh-
quah,* being at the East end of Nantucket, for and in
consideration of five pounds to be paid to me in Eng-

---

* Pocomo.

lish goods, or otherwise to my content by the same
Tristram Coffin aforesaid at convenient time as shall
be demanded.

"Witness my hand or mark this 22 of June 1662.
                              WANACKMAMAK.

"Witness hereto, Peter Folger and Wawinnesit
whose English name is Amos."

*"Copy of Indian deed of Nantucket, Recorded for Mr.
Tristram Coffin and Mr. Thomas Macy, ye 29th of
June 1671 aforesaid.*

"These P^rsents Wittness y^t I Wanackmamack Head
Sachem of ye Island of Nantuckett, have Bargained
and sold, and doe by these Presents Bargaine and Sell
unto Tristram Coffin, Thomas Macy, Richd Swayne,
Thomas Bernard, John Swain, Mr Thomas Mayhew,
Edward Starbuck, Peter Coffin, James Coffin, Stephen
Greenleafe, Tristram Coffin Junr, Thomas Coleman,
Robert Bernard, Christopher Hussey, Robert Pyke,
John Smyth, and John Bishop these Islands of Nan-
tucket, namely, all ye west end of ye afores^d Island
unto ye Pond comonly called Waquittaquay and from
ye Head of that Pond to ye North side of ye Island
Manamoy; Bounded by a Path from ye Head of ye
Pond aforesaid to Manamoy; as also a Neck at y^e
East End of ye Island called Poquomock,* wth the
Property thereof, and all ye Royaltyes, Priviledges and
Immunityes thereto belonging, or whatsoever Right I
ye afores^d Wanackmak have, or have had in ye same:
That is, all ye Lands afore menconed and likewise ye
Winter sseed of ye whole island from ye End of an In-
dyan Harvest untill Planting Time, or ye first of May,

* Pocomo.

from yeare to yeare forever, as likewise Liberty to make use of Wood and Timber on all Parts of y⁰ Island; and likewise Halfe of y⁰ Meadows and Marshes on all Parts of y⁰ Island wᵗʰout or beside y⁰ afores⁴ tracts of Land Purchased; And likewise y⁰ use of y⁰ other Halfe of y⁰ Meadows and Marshes, as long as y⁰ aforesaid English their Heyres or Assignes live on ye Island; And likewise I the aforesaid Wanackmamack doe sell unto y⁰ English afore menconed y⁰ propriety of y⁰ rest of y⁰ Island belonging unto mee, for and in consideracon of fforty Pounds already received by mee or other by my Consent or Ord.

"To Have and to hold, ye afores⁴ Tracts of Land, wᵗʰ y⁰ P'priety, Royaltyies, Immunityes, Priviledges, and all Appertenances thereunto belonging to them y⁰ afores⁴ Purchasᵐ their Heyres and Assignes forever.

"In witness Whereof I the afores⁴ Wanackmamack have hereunto sett my Hand and Seale y⁰ Daye and Yeare above written.

"The Sign of Wanack-Mamack.

"Signed, Sealed and Delivered
    in y⁰ p'sence of
"Peter Foulger,
"Eleazer Foulger,
"Dorcas Starbuck." *

RECEIPT OF WANACKMAMACK.

(*Nantucket Records, Old Book, Page 27.*)

"Received of Tristram Coffin of Nantuckett, the just sume of five poun, which is part of the seven

---

* Dorcas Starbuck was a daughter of Edward Starbuck. Eleazer Foulger was a son of Peter Foulger.

Note.—The official records of these deeds are in the office of the Secretary of State, Albany, New York.

poun that was unpaid of the Twenty poun Purchase
of the Land that was purchased of Wanackmamack
and Neckanoose, that is to say from Monomoy to
Waquettaquage pond, Nanahumack Neck and all from
Wesco westward to the west end of Nantucket, I say
Received by Me Wanackmamack of Tristram Coffin,
five pounds Starling the 18th 11 M 1671

> " The Mark × of Wanackmamack.
" Witness hereunto
" RICHARD GARDNER.
" ELEZER FOLGER."

The following Associates were chosen by the first
Proprietors :

TRISTRAM COFFIN, JR.	JOHN SMITH.
ROBERT PIKE.	ROBERT BARNARD.
THOMAS COLEMAN.	EDWARD STARBUCK.
NATHANIEL STARBUCK.	THOMAS LOOK.
JAMES COFFIN.	THOMAS MAYHEW, JR.

They purchased or were given a half-interest in the
original apportionments, making at a very early date
twenty landed proprietors.

Among these were men of varied experience and
marked executive ability, evinced by their embracing
every opportunity for the advancement of the settlement, and soon an interesting society was established
upon the island.

The first houses were built at the northwest, not far
from a small harbor now called Maddequet Harbor.

Later the large harbor on the north side of the
island offered decided advantages, and the town was
finally located there and named Sherburne, in com-

pliance with written orders of Governor Lovelace, of New York, recorded in Albany in the Secretary's office in Book of Deeds III. p. 85. Many of the houses were moved from their original sites to the new town.

Numbers at first were so small that intermarriages among these families were very common, and it is not infrequent for a descendant to find the same settler in his family tree several times.

The population increased steadily until about 1849, when the California gold fever led many to seek wealth on the Pacific Coast, and later, the decline of the whale fisheries compelled the younger men to find means of support elsewhere, and in comparatively few years the population decreased from nearly ten thousand to less than five thousand.

THOMAS MACY.

NEAR the town of Salisbury, in Wiltshire, England, in the Parish of Chilmark, resided ("prior to his embarkation for America, probably in 1635") Thomas Macy.

The name of the vessel upon which he came to America is not recorded, but he arrived not later than 1639.

Thomas Macy was among the original settlers of Salisbury, Massachusetts, and is in "The first or Original list of ye townsmen of Salisbury in y° booke of Records."

We find also recorded that he was "a merchant, planter,* one of the select-men of the town, a juryman, and, withal a preacher."

The Massachusetts laws passed in 1656 and 1657 were a great drawback to freedom of worship.

Several persons were prosecuted for violating the law of 1657 which prohibited entertaining Quakers. Among these was Thomas Macy, who was fined thirty shillings, notwithstanding his "explanation and apology," and was ordered to be admonished by the governor.

It is a matter of record that he sheltered Edward Wharton, William Robinson, merchant of London, and Marmaduke Stephenson, of Yorkshire, England. The two last named were hanged in Boston the 27th of October, 1659.

The following letter from General Court files is a copy of a reply to a summons to appear at court to answer for his violation of the law in this particular:

* A farmer.

2

" This is to entreat the honored Court not to be offended because of my non-appearance. It is not from any slighting the authority of this honored Court, nor from feare to answer the case, but I have bin for some weeks past very ill, and am so at present, and notwithstanding my illness, yet I desirous to appear, have done my utmost endeavour to hire a horse but cannot procure one at present.

" I being at present destitute have endeavoured to purchase, but at present cannot attaine it, but shall relate the truth of the case as my answer should be to y⁰ honored Court, and more cannot be proved, nor so much.

" On a rainy morning there came to my house Edward Wharton and three men more, the said Wharton spoke to me saying that they were travelling eastward and desired me to direct them in the way to Hampton, and asked me how far it was to Casco Bay.

" I never saw any of y⁰ men afore except Wharton neither did I require their names, or who they were, but by their carriage I thought they might be Quakers and told them so, and therefore desired them to passe on their way, saying to them I might possibly give offence in entertaining them, and as soone as the violence of the rain ceased (for it rained very hard) they went away and I never saw them since.

" The time that they stayed in the house was about three quarters of an hour, but I can safely affirm that it was not an houre.

" They spake not many words in the time, neither was I at leisure to talke with them, for I came home wet to y⁰ skin, immediately afore they came to the house and I found my wife sick in bed. If this satisfie not the honored Court I shall subject to their sentence.

"I have not willingly offended. I am ready to serve and obey you in the Lord.

"THOS. MACY."

He was a Baptist, and on the Sabbath frequently exhorted the people; this, too, was in violation of the Massachusetts law which prohibited all but the regularly ordained from such service.

Tradition says that immediately after his sentence Thomas Macy removed to Nantucket.

In the "Macy Genealogy" it is related that "in 1659 he embarked at Salisbury in a small boat with his wife and children and such household goods as he could conveniently carry, and in company with Isaac Coleman and Edward Starbuck set sail for Nantucket." *

The same papers say, "because he could not in justice to the dictates of his own conscious longer submit to the tyranny of the clergy and those in authority."

It appears from the above detail that Thomas Macy satisfied the requirements of the law and paid his fine, but undoubtedly he believed he could lead a more peaceful and independent life at Nantucket, and may have preferred voluntary exile to possible banishment.

Thomas Macy must have returned to Salisbury, as he is recorded as living there in 1664.

Before his removal to Nantucket he was commissioner, and representative to the General Court from Salisbury, and the citizens of that town bore testimony of their sympathy with him by electing his friend and defender Robert Pike as his successor.

That he again, at a later date, removed to Nantucket is evident from old records, Register's office, in which

* James Coffin, son of Tristram, Sr., is said to have accompanied the three named.

it will be found that October 1, 1675, he was commissioned chief magistrate of the town.

He was the first recorder appointed on the island, and a portion at least of the first Book of Records in the office at Nantucket was written by him.

He died April 19, 1682, aged seventy-four. His wife, Sarah (Hopcot) Macy, who came with him from Chilmark, survived him for nearly a quarter of a century.

JOHN MACY, son of Thomas and Sarah Macy, born at Salisbury July 14, 1655, married Deborah Gardner, daughter of Richard and Sarah (Shattuck) Gardner, and died at Nantucket, October 14, 1691, at the early age of thirty-six; through him alone the name has descended to posterity.

Note.—In 1637–88, GEORGE MACY appears to have been prominent in the settlement of Taunton, Massachusetts. Savage (vol. iii. p. 142) says he was in 1643 lieutenant in King Philip's War, and representative in 1672 and for six years; also among the inhabitants of Taunton in 1668 there was a Samuel Macy, who is supposed to have been a son of George and to have died single prior to the death of his father; of this Taunton family there is no further record, nor of any others of the name excepting Thomas and his descendants.

The only reasons for supposing George Macy was of the same family as Thomas are the name and the date of his emigration to America.

The name Macy signifies mace or staff.

EDWARD STARBUCK.

EDWARD STARBUCK was born in 1604, and came from Derbyshire, England, to Dover, New Hampshire, with his wife, Katharine (Reynolds), of Wales, about 1635.

"He is first mentioned as receiving 1643 a grant of forty acres of land on each side of the Fresh River at Cutchechoe . . . and also one platt of Marsh above Cutchechoe great Marsh, that the brook that runs out of the river runs through, first discovered by Richard Walderne, Edward Colcord, Edward Starbuck, and William Furber.

"He had other grants at different times, one of Marsh in Great Bay in 1643, one of the Mill privilege at Cutchechoe 2nd Falls (with Thomas Wiggins) and one of timber to 'accommodate' in 1650 and various others.

"Indeed Edward owned considerable land and was evidently a man of substance as to possessions as tradition says he was in body.

"He was a representative in 1643 and 1646, was an elder in the church and enjoyed various other tokens of respect given him by his fellow citizens.

"In fact he might have lived comfortably at Dover and died in the midst of his family, respected and contented but that he embraced Baptist sentiments." *

In Provincial "Papers of New Hampshire Historical Society," we find the following:

"Oct. 18, 1648.—The Court being informed of great misdemeanor Committed by Edward Starbuck of Dover with profession of Anabatism for which he is to be proceeded against at the next Court of Assistants if evi-

---

* N. E. Hist. and Gen. Reg., vol. viii. p. 68.

dence can be prepared by that time & it being very farre for witnesses to travill to Boston at that season of the year, It is therefore ordered by this Court that the Secretary shall give Commission to Capt. Thomas Wiggan & Mr Edw. Smyth to send for such persons as they shall have notice of which are able to testify in the sd. cause & to take their testimony uppon oath & certifie the same to the secretary so soon as may be, that further proceedings may be therein, if the cause shall so require"

It is not to be wondered at that Edward Starbuck was quite ready to leave Dover under existing conditions. He was fifty-five years of age when he joined Thomas Macy in his voyage from Salisbury to Nantucket; he spent the winter there and in the spring returned to Dover for his family, who all accompanied him to the island excepting his daughters Sarah (Austin) and Abigail (Coffin), who had married and settled in Dover. "Dover lost a good citizen" and Nantucket gained a much respected one; "he was a leading man on the Island and at one time a Magistrate;" * he is described as " courageous and persevering."

In " Landmarks in Ancient Dover" mention is made of Starbuck's Brook in 1701 as a boundary of property which Peter Coffin (son-in-law of Edward Starbuck) conveyed to John Ham. Starbuck's Marsh was granted to Elder Starbuck August 30, 1643, and Starbuck's Point and Marsh, now called Fabyan's Point, was granted to Edward Starbuck in 1643, and is again mentioned in 1662, 1702, and 1716 in conveyance of property, since which time the usual desire to change

---

* N. E. Hist. and Gen. Reg., vol. viii. p. 68.

ancient names has destroyed what might be valuable historical landmarks.

One son only lived to perpetuate the name,—Nathaniel, who married Mary (daughter of Tristram Coffin); he is the ancestor of all American Starbucks.

Edward Starbuck died in 1690.

Note.—The name Starbuck is from the Norse, and signifies great or grand.

TRISTRAM COFFIN.

So much information concerning Tristram Coffin has been developed and published in connection with the Coffin Reunion at Nantucket in 1881, that a very brief sketch is sufficient here.

He was so important in the early history of the settlement that at the risk of repeating much that has already been written, some notice of him and his interesting family will not be out of place.

Tristram Coffin, the founder of the family line of Coffins in America signed his name " Coffyn."

He was born in Brixton, Devonshire, England, in 1605. He married Dionis Stevens, daughter of Robert Stevens, of Brixton.

In 1642 he came to America with his family and his widowed mother Joan, and resided first at Newbury, later at Haverhill and Salisbury, until 1660, when he settled at Nantucket.

The family to which he belonged is the oldest of the Nantucket families. The first of the name of whom there is any record is Sir Richard Coffin, who removed from Normandy to England in 1066; he entered the

---

Note.—Coffin is a word of Hebrew origin signifying a small basket. In the "Century Dictionary" may be found various meanings for the word, but in most cases it represents a receptacle of some kind.

In Wyclif's translation of the Bible, Mark vi. 43, may be found: "And thei token the relifs of broken metis twelve coffinsful and of the fisches."

Coffin also appears to have been at one time synonymous with coffer; there are occasional records where the cofferer was a treasurer, an official servant in charge of a receptacle in which valuables and money were placed for transportation from place to place.

In Bowditch's "Suffolk Surnames" the name Tristram is spoken of as having been a surname.

English army, had lands granted to him, and was knighted by the king.

From Prince's "Worthies of Devonshire" we learn that the ancient family of the name settled at Portledge, by the sea-side, in the Parish of Alwington, five miles from Biddeford, "and flourished there from the time of King Henry the First unto the age of King Edward the Second."

For two hundred years each successive heir of this family bore the name of Richard.

Within a short distance of Fallaise, a town of Normandy, stands the old château of Cortiton, once the home of the Norman Coffins.

The last Miss Coffin married a Le Clerc late in the eighteenth century, since which time the Le Clerc family has occupied the Norman estates. When last visited, the château, though ancient, was in good repair.

Members of the family are mentioned in history often associated with royalty from 1066 to the latter part of the sixteenth century, since which time the lines of descent are complete.

Tristram lived at Northam,* near Capaum Pond, Nantucket, and died tenth month 2d, 1681, aged seventy-six years.

He was the first chief magistrate of Nantucket. The following is a copy of his commission, taken from Mr. F. B. Hough's book, compiled from official records at Albany.

---

* Northam was the first name of Dover, New Hampshire.

" Commiſſion Granted to Mr. Tristram Coffin, Senr., to be Chiefe Magiſtrate in and over the Iſlands of Nantuckett and Tuckanuckett."—[*Deeds III., 62, Secretary's Office, Albany, New York.*

"Francis Lovelace, Esq., &c : Whereas upon Addreſs made unto mee by Mr. Triſtram Coffin and Mr. Thomas Macy on yᵉ behalfe of themſelves and yᵉ reſt of yᵉ Inhabitants of Nantuckett Iſland concerning yᵉ Mannoʳ and Method of Governmnᵗ to be uſed amongſᵗ themſelves, and having by yᵉ Advice of my Councell pitcht upon a way for them ; That is to ſay That they be Governed by a Perſon as Chiefe Magiſtrate, and two Aſſiſtants, yᵉ former to be nominated by myſelfe, yᵉ other to bee choſen and confirmed by yᵉ Inhabitants as in yᵉ Inſtructions ſent unto them is more particularly Sett forth. And having conceived a good Opinion of yᵉ ffitneſs and capacity of Mr. Triſtram Coffin to be yᵉ pʳſent Chiefe Magiſtrate to manage Affayres wᵗʰ yᵉ Ayd and good Advice of yᵉ Aſſiſtants in yᵉ Islands of Nantuckett and Tuckanuckett, I have thought fitt to Nominate, Conſtitute, and Appoint and by these Pʳſents doe hereby Nominate Conſtitute and Appoint Mr. Triſtram Coffin to be Chiefe Magiſtrate of yᵉ ſaid Iſlands of Nantuckett and Tuckanuckett. In yᵉ Managemᵗ of wᶜʰ ſaid Employmᵗ, hee is to uſe his beſt Skill and Endeavour to pʳſerve his Maᵗⁱᵉˢ Peace, and to keep yᵉ Inhabitants in good Ordʳ. And all Persons are hereby required to give yᵉ ſaid Mr. Triſtram Coffin ſuch Reſpect and Obedience as belongs to a Person inveſted by commiſſion from Authority of his Royall Ilighneſs in yᵉ Place and Employmᵗ of a Chief Magistrate in yᵉ Iſlands aforeſaid. And hee is duely to obſerve the Orders and Inſtructions wᶜʰ are already given forth for y⁰ well governing of y⁰ Place, or fuch others as from Time to Time fhall hereafter bee given by mee : And for whatfoever y⁰ faid Mr. Triftram Coffin fhall lawfully Act or Doe in Profecution of y⁰ Premifes, This is my Commiffion wch is to bee of fforce untill y⁰ 13th day of October, which shall bee in ye Yeare of our Lord 1672, when a new magiftrate is to enter into the Employm⁰ fhall bee his sufficient Warrant and Difcharge.

"Given under my Hand and Seal at fforte James in New Yorke, this 29th day of June in y⁰ 22^d Yeare of his Maties Reigne, Annoq. Dni. 1671.

"FRAN: LOVELACE."

The following is a list of children of Tristram Coffin :

HON. PETER COFFIN was born in England in 1631; he married Abigail Starbuck, daughter of Edward and Katharine Starbuck, of Dover, New Hampshire. He was one of the original purchasers of Nantucket, but resided there for a short time only. He was made a freeman in 1666 at Dover.

In 1675 he was a lieutenant on service in King Philip's War. In 1672–73 and again in 1679 he was a representative in the legislative branch. In 1690 he removed to Exeter, New Hampshire. From 1692 to 1714 he was at different times associate justice and chief justice of the Supreme Court of New Hampshire, and a member of the Governor's Council. He died at Exeter, March 21, 1715.

TRISTRAM COFFIN, JR., was born in England in 1632. He married in Newbury, Massachusetts, March 2, 1652, Judith Somerby, widow of Henry Somerby and daughter of Edmund and Sarah Greenleaf. He

28

was made freeman April 29, 1668, and died in Newbury, Febuary 4, 1704, aged seventy-two. He was a
merchant tailor and filled many positions of trust. He
lived in the Coffin mansion in Newbury, which still
continues in the family; whether he or his wife's
former husband built it is uncertain.

It is said that Tristram Coffin, Sr., lived in this old
mansion before he removed to Nantucket.

ELIZABETH COFFIN was born in England about
1634–35; and married in Newbury, November 13,
1651, Captain Stephen Greenleaf, son of Edmund
Greenleaf; she died at Newbury, November 19, 1678.

JAMES COFFIN was born in England, August 12,
1640. He married, December 3, 1663, Mary, daughter
of John and Abigail Severance, of Salisbury, Massachusetts, and died at Nantucket, July 28, 1720, aged
eighty years. He was one of the associate proprietors,
and filled several important offices at Nantucket,
among them judge of Probate Court, and is said to
have been the first judge of probate on the island,
appointed in 1680.*

JOHN and DEBORAH died in infancy.

MARY COFFIN, seventh child of Tristram Coffin, Sr.,
was born in Haverhill, February 20, 1645. She was
married in 1662, at the age of seventeen, to Nathaniel,
son of Edward and Katharine (Reynolds) Starbuck.

The first book of births, marriages, and deaths for
the town of Sherburne (page 11) says " Mary Starbuck

---

* Massachusetts Civil List, pp. 112–114.

departed this Liffe y 13 day of y 9$\frac{o}{m}$ 1717 in y 74 year of her age and was decently buried in Friends burying ground." Her husband, Nathaniel Starbuck, Sr., died in 1719.

She was a remarkable woman, anticipating by two centuries the advanced views of women of to-day. She took an active part in town debates, usually opening her remarks with " My husband and I, having considered the subject, think, etc."

In 1701, at the age of fifty-six, she became interested in the religious faith of the Friends, and held meetings at her house. She was a minister in the Society, as were also several of her children, her grandsons Elihu and Nathaniel Coleman, and her grand-daughter Priscilla Bunker.

Elihu Coleman published one of the earliest protests against slavery in New England.

Mary Starbuck was " as distinguished in her domestic economy as she was celebrated as a preacher."

The following copy of a letter from Mary Starbuck to her grand-daughter Eliza Gorham, who had suffered loss by fire, gives evidence of her interest in domestic matters.

"NANTUCKET 17th of 1st mo 1714.

" DEAR CHILD E. G.

" These few lines may certify thee that thou art often in my remembrance, with thy dear husband and children, with breathings to the Lord for you, that you may find rest in all your visitations and trials; As also that there is a trunk filled with goods which is intended to be put on Eben Stewards vessel, in which are several small tokens from thy friends which thou may particularly see by the little invoices here enclosed, and by some other marks that are upon the things.

"Thy Aunt Dorcas in a new pair of osnaburg sheets, thy Aunt Dinah in a pair of blankets, Thy Grandfather intends to send thee a bbl. of mutton, but it is not all his own, for Cousin James Coffin sent hither 17 pieces. Cousin James said he intended to send thee two or three bushels of corn.

"There is likewise sent from our women's meeting £7 which thy uncle Jethro said he would give an order for, for thee to take to Boston.

"Sister James told me she intended to send thee two bushels of corn and some wool and likewise that Justice Worth said he would send thee some corn.

"More meat and corn will be sent which will be in greater quantities, which thy uncle Jethro Starbuck will give thee an acct. of or to thy husband.

"I should have been glad if he had come over with Steward, but I hope we shall see him this summer, if not both of you.

"So with my kind love to thee and thy husband, children and to all our frds. committing you to the protection of the Almighty who is the wise disposer of all things and remain thy affectionate Grandmother

"MARY STARBUCK.

"Thy Grandfather's love to you all and Uncle Barnabas's, Susanna is well and her love to you also."

Nathaniel Starbuck was in his time considered wealthy, and was by no means a man of small ability, but his wife seems to have taken the lead in most matters.

LIEUTENANT JOHN COFFIN was born at Haverhill, October 30, 1647; he married Deborah, daughter of Joseph and Sarah (Starbuck) Austin. After his father's

death he removed to Martha's Vineyard, and died there
September 5, 1711.

Authority for his commission as lieutenant of militia
will be found Part First of Vol. XXXIV., and on page
21 of the New York Colonial Manuscripts in the custody of the Regents of the University in the State Li-
brary at Albany, and recorded by the Secretary of the
Province of New York among memoranda of several
military commissions, directed by Governor Thomas
Dongan to be issued, and reads thus:

"Mr. John Coffin a Commission to be Lieu. of said
Company at Nantucket June 5th 1684 all the first
forme."

STEPHEN COFFIN was born at Newbury, May 10, 1652.
He married Mary, daughter of George and Jane (God-
frey) Bunker, about 1668, and died at Nantucket
November 14, 1734.

He remained upon his father's estate, and to him
was given the management of his father's business, on
agreement "to be helpful to his parents in their old age."

It is not surprising that the descendants of Tristram
Coffin still bearing the name are so numerous when
we find that of his nine children five out of the seven
who married were sons; that Peter had nine children,
that Tristram, Jr., had ten children and left one hundred and seventy-seven descendants, that James had
fourteen children, that Lieutenant John had eleven
children, and that Stephen had ten.

The two daughters, Mary Starbuck and Elizabeth
Greenleaf, each had ten children, adding in two centuries many more descendants to the list, although not
of the name.

The Nantucket *Inquirer* of July 22, 1826, says, "The House * in which Tristram Coffin resided is still standing, and has been the residence of seven generations of the same name.

"The names of more than twelve thousand descendants of Tristram Coffin can be ascertained, some of whom are found in England, in all the British Dominions and in every state in the Union."

The above was written by Joshua Coffin,† Newburyport, and is signed "Jam satis."

---

* Probably at Newbury.

† Joshua Coffin, antiquarian and historian, was descended from Joseph, son of Nathaniel, who was youngest son of Tristram Coffin, Jr.

Joseph married Margaret Morse, daughter of Benjamin Morse, of Newbury.

"Joshua Coffin, Esq.," was born in the old Coffin mansion in Newbury, October 12, 1792, and died June 24, 1864. He was one of the twelve persons who, together with William Lloyd Garrison and others, formed the first anti-slavery society in New England. He was for many years a teacher, and numbered among his pupils men who attained high position in after years.

Note.—Savage says, "Twenty-six of Tristram's descendants graduated in 1828 at New England colleges, fifteen at Harvard alone."

ADMIRAL SIR ISAAC COFFIN, BARONET.

The following facts have been abridged from an account published in the Boston *Herald* within a few years.

On the easterly side of Harrison Avenue just above Kneeland Street, a trifle back from the Avenue (Boston), stands a gambrel roof wooden structure. This building was moved from its original site, corner of Beach Street and Oxford Place, to its present location nearly half a century ago. It was the residence of Nathaniel Coffin, one of the foremost adherents of King George, who at one time held the responsible position of collector of his Majesty's customs for the port of Boston. The house must have been built as early as 1750, and it was, on May 16, 1759, the birthplace of Isaac Coffin, who afterwards rose to be an admiral in the British navy. In the same house was born his brother John, who became major-general in the British army.

Sir Isaac retained an affection for the place of his birth, and coming from Nantucket stock he invested in 1827 the sum of £2500 in English funds for the establishment of a school on that Island to be known as the "Coffin School."

Drake, in his "Old Landmarks of Boston," says that of this fund "the Mayor and Aldermen of Boston were made trustees for the distribution of the annual interest among five of the most deserving boys and as many girls of that school."

King George III., with whom Sir Isaac was a great favorite, gave him a grant of the Island of Magdalen in the Gulf of St. Lawrence, and in after years it was proposed to create him Earl of Magdalen; this proposition fell through, and the alleged reason was, that in establishing the Coffin school in Nantucket he was creating sailors who in mature age might fight against the crown.

At the present time the old house in Boston is used for manufacturing purposes.

Sir Isaac Coffin was the fifth generation in descent from Tristram, Sr., his father being Nathaniel, who married Elizabeth, daughter of Henry Barnes, of Boston. Nathaniel was the son of William, who was the son of Nathaniel, who was the son of James, who was the son of Tristram Coffin, Sr.

The following extracts from an English biographical work on the life of Admiral Coffin are abridged from manuscript of the late Mr. George Howland Folger. This manuscript is now the property of the Historical Society of Nantucket.

Sir Isaac entered the navy in 1773, under the patronage of Admiral John Montague; he served as midshipman on board several ships, and in 1778 obtained a lieutenancy. In July, 1781, he was promoted to the rank of commander, and was in the "splendid battle" of April 12, 1782, which resulted in the capture of the celebrated Comte de Grasse. In 1795, as commissioner, he resided in Corsica, where he remained until the evacuation of the island in 1796; here he twice narrowly escaped assassination. After passing through various fortunes of war, he was in 1804 made rear-admiral. Soon after this he was raised to the dignity of baronet. In 1808 he was promoted to the position of vice-admiral, and in 1814 became full admiral, and in the general election in 1818 was chosen as representative to Parliament for the borough of Ilchester.

He married, in 1811, at the age of fifty-two, Elizabeth Brown Greenly, only daughter of T. Greenly, Esq. There were no children.

He crossed the Atlantic not less than thirty-one times, a circumstance more remarkable in the early part of the century than at present.

In the Nantucket *Inquirer* of September 2, 1826, may be found the following, copied from a Boston paper :

"According to previous appointment, the annual visitation of the public schools was attended on Wednesday last by the parents and friends of the pupils, and by several strangers of distinction. Admiral Coffin gave as a sentiment, 'The City of Boston.'

"He was replied to by one of the committee.

"Our venerable and respected guest, Admiral Coffin, a native of our city and an alumnus of our ancient Latin school, who, though separated from us, in times of political dissension was generous and kind to his countrymen, who amidst the honors and plaudits of a princely court remembered with affection the land of his birth, and still bears testimony to the excellence of our civil and literary institutions.

"May honorable fame ever attend him, and may his declining years repose in health and peace."

September 9, 1826.—"Honorary degree of M.A. was conferred on Admiral Sir Isaac Coffin at the annual commencement of Harvard University."

In the Nantucket *Inquirer* of date September 16, 1826, there is a notice of a visit of Sir Isaac Coffin to Nantucket, during which he spoke with affection of his native city, and attributed "all his attainments and renown to principles of knowledge imbibed in the public schools of Boston."

During his stay on the island he " visited principal places of resort, disregarded all court etiquette, and mingled freely with the inhabitants."

He died at Cheltenham, England, in 1839, aged eighty years.

CHRISTOPHER HUSSEY.

CHRISTOPHER HUSSEY was baptized in Dorking, Surrey, England, and was the son of John Hussey and Mary (Wood).

When a young man he spent some time in Holland, where he solicited in marriage Theodate, daughter of Rev. Stephen Batchilder, who gave his consent to their union on condition that they would come to America with him; this condition was complied with, and they arrived in Boston in 1632 on the ship William and Francis.

Christopher Hussey was one of the original settlers of Hampton, New Hampshire; in 1636 he was " chosen by papers" as one of the " seven men," as they were first called, then " towncsmen," then " townesmen select," and finally " select men," as at present.

" They were fully empowered of themselves to do what the town had power to do, the reason whereof was the town judged it inconvenient and burdensome to be called together upon every occasion."

In 1639, Christopher Hussey was made Justice of the Peace, which office he held several years; he was also town clerk and one of the first deacons of the church.*

In 1659 he became one of the purchasers of Nantucket; subsequently he was a sea-captain.

Orders were received from the king, September 18, 1679, " to erect New Hampshire into a separate government," under jurisdiction of a president and council to be appointed by himself; John Cutts was appointed president and Christopher Hussey, of Hampton, one of six councillors.†

---

* Savage's General Dictionary.
† One Hundred and Sixty Allied Families, p. 146.

There are several theories concerning the death of Christopher Hussey. The fact that he followed the sea may have given rise to a belief that he was drowned at sea or eaten by cannibals. Joshua Coffin, however, says that he *died* at Hampton, New Hampshire, March 6, 1686, and Austin, in " One Hundred and Sixty Allied Families," states that " Town records of Hampton declare he was buried there March 8, 1686."

He had three sons and three daughters :

Stephen, married Martha Bunker.

John, married Rebecca Perkins.

Joseph.

Hulda, married John Smith and lived to be ninety-seven years old.

Mary.

Theodata.

His eldest son, Stephen, who was born in Lynn, and was the first child christened there by his grandfather Rev. Stephen Batchilder, came to Nantucket and married Martha Bunker, October 8, 1676. He had lived at Barbadoes, had considerable property, and was a Friend before a Society was formed upon the island.

Note—REV. STEPHEN BATCHILDER, or Bachiler, settled in Lynn, Massachusetts, in 1632, and with a few others established a church ; he was its first pastor. (Savage's General Dictionary, and One Hundred and Sixty Allied Families.)

His signature and seal appended to letters may be seen in Massachusetts Historical Collection, vol. vii., fourth series.

His children were :

Theodata Batchilder, married Christopher Hussey.

Deborah Batchilder, married John Wing.

—— Batchilder, married —— Sanborn, and had :

> John Sanborn.
> Stephen Sanborn.
> William Sanborn.

He was at one time representative to the General Court.

He died February 2, 1718, in his eighty-eighth year, and was buried in Friends' first burial ground at Nantucket. His children were Puella, Abigail, Sylvanus, Bachiller, Daniel, George, and Theodata.

Nathaniel Batchilder, married 1st, Deborah Smith; 2d, Mary Wyman, of Woburn.

Francis Batchilder.

Stephen Batchilder.

Some old records name a daughter Abigail Bachiler, who married Richard Austin, father of Joseph.

Rev. Stephen Batchelder was also one of the early settlers of Hampton, New Hampshire.

"The first churches were formed at Hampton and Exeter. Hampton claims precedence in time. . . . The first pastor of this first-born church of the New State, and the father of the town, was Rev. Stephen Bachiler, an ancestor on the mother's side of Daniel Webster." (History of New Hampshire, by Edwin L Sanborn, LL.D., p. 58.)

STEPHEN GREENLEAF, WITH SOME ACCOUNT OF HIS FATHER, EDMUND GREENLEAF.

THE Greenleaf family is supposed to have been of Huguenot origin. The name was first known in England in 1590.

Edmund, the first of the name who came to America, was born in the parish of Brixham, about 1600. He married Sarah Dole, and with several children settled in Newburyport, Massachusetts, in 1635.

In 1639 he was made ensign, and later, lieutenant, and removed from Newbury to Boston.*

Captain Johnson styles Edmund Greenleaf an "ancient and experienced lieutenant under Captain Gerrish, in 1644."

The following is an extract from his will: "my will is being according to God's will and revealed in his word, that wee must pay what we owe and live of the rest, unto whose rule the sons of men ought to frame their wills and actions therefore." This to show his correct principles. Another extract may be given, showing how absolute he considered his power over his wife, who evidently had a will of her own:

". . . Besides when I married my wife she brought me a silver bowl, a silver porringer, a silver spoon, she lent or gave them to her son-in-law, James Hill, without my consent."

This will is dated December 25, 1668.

STEPHEN GREENLEAF, son of Edmund, was born in 1630, and married, November 13, 1651, Elizabeth Coffin, daughter of Tristram Coffin and Dionis (Stevens) Coffin.

---

* Colonial Records.

He was one of the original proprietors of Nantucket, and, authority says, " a religious man."

He was ensign, 1686, and captain in 1690, and engaged in Indian wars; he was also representative to the General Court in 1676.

At a court held at Newbury in 1686, March 30, " David Pierce, Captain Thomas Noyes, and Lieutenant Stephen Greenleaf are commissioned to be Magistrates by the Court."

" In the same year Lieutenant Stephen Greenleaf and Lieutenant Tristram Coffin with others are appointed a committee on laying out and dividing woodlands."

November 21, 1686, " deacon Nicolas Noyes, deacon Robert Long and deacon Tristram Coffin were at the request of the select men chosen standing overseers of the poore for the town of Newbury."

December 1, " Captain Daniel Pierce and Captain Stephen Greenleaf were added to the deacons as overseers of the poore," and any three of them had power to act.

May 6, 1689, " The Committee of Safety in Boston having desired us to send a man or men for consulting with them what may be best for the conservation of the peace of the country, Our inhabitants being met this 6th day of May, 1689, have chosen Captain Thomas Noyes and lieutenant Stephen Greenleaf sen. for the end aforesaid."

March 5, 1696, Captain Greenleaf petitions the General Court for compensation for repulsing an Indian raid, in which he was wounded in his side and wrist.

His petition was read and forty pounds voted to be paid him out of the treasury of the province.

The house attacked by the Indians was John Brown's,

and the following is the family tradition respecting it :

" The Indians had secreted themselves for sometime near the house, waiting for the absence of the male members of the family, who about three o'clock departed with a load of turnips. The Indians then rushed from their concealment, tomahawked a girl who was standing at the front door; another girl who had concealed herself as long as the Indians remained, immediately after their departure gave the alarm."

The coat which Captain Greenleaf wore in his pursuit of the Indians is still preserved by his descendants, together with the bullet which was extracted from his wound.

With nine others, Stephen Greenleaf was wrecked and drowned off Cape Breton, December 1, 1690.

Note.—State Street in Newbury (now Newburyport) was formerly Greenleaf's Lane.

JOHN GREENLEAF WHITTIER.

THE blood of more than one of the pioneers of Nantucket flowed in the veins of the poet Whittier.

The descent from Christopher Hussey, which was a tradition of the Whittier family, and was believed by the poet himself, appears upon late investigation to be uncertain. Recently, antiquarians trace his ancestry to Robert Hussey, who possibly was a son of Christopher, but this is not probable.

His biographer, Mr. S. T. Pickard, of Portland, Maine, himself a descendant of Tristram Coffin, and a nephew of Joshua Coffin, the historian, is authority for the following statement.

The lines of descent are complete from Tristram Coffin and Stephen Greenleaf, and are as follows:

Edmund Greenleaf married Sarah Dole, and their son, Stephen Greenleaf, married Elizabeth, daughter of Tristram Coffin and Dionis (Stevens). The son of Stephen Greenleaf and Elizabeth (Coffin)—viz.: Tristram Greenleaf, born in 1667—married Margaret Piper in 1689; Tristram Greenleaf's son, Nathaniel Greenleaf, born in 1691, had a daughter Sarah, born March 5, 1721; she married Joseph Whittier, 2d, the grandfather of the poet.

OTHER PROPRIETORS.

RECORDED details of the remaining proprietors are very brief; concerning some there appears to be little record excepting of their proprietorship.

ROBERT PIKE was one of the original settlers of Salisbury, Massachusetts, and shared the interest of Christopher Hussey as a proprietor of Nantucket. He continued his relations with the settlers of the island until his death, which occurred about forty years after the purchase. As has already been stated, he was the warm friend of Thomas Macy.

In 1637, on the 17th of May, in order to prevent the re-election of Sir Harry Vane as governor, and to strengthen the friends of Winthrop, ten men, among them Robert Pike and Thomas Coleman, went from Newbury to Cambridge on foot (forty miles) and qualified themselves to vote by taking the freeman's oath. Winthrop was chosen governor. (N. E. Hist. and Gen. Reg.)

Robert Pike was representative to the General Court in 1648–49 and 1658–59; captain and major in 1670; an assistant in 1682; and a member of the Council of Safety in 1689.

THOMAS COLEMAN must have removed to Nantucket prior to 1673, as on October 20 of that year he is recorded as "drawn on the jury" there. He is also named with Christopher Hussey and others in a list of those who settled Hampton, New Hampshire.

Note.—Davis's History of Bucks County says the Pike family of Bucks County, Pennsylvania, is said to descend from Robert Pike of Massachusetts.

THOMAS and ROBERT BARNARD * settled in America about 1650. Thomas was one of the purchasers of Nantucket, in 1659; he transferred one-half of his interest to his brother Robert Barnard. Thomas died abroad. Robert Barnard, of Salisbury, Massachusetts, removed to Nantucket in 1663, and died there in 1682; he married Joanna Harvey, who died in 1705; he had a son, John Barnard, born in 1642, who married Bethiah Folger, daughter of Peter Folger, and a daughter, Mary Barnard, who married her cousin Nathaniel Barnard, son of Thomas and Eleanor Barnard.

Among prominent men who have had a claim on Nantucket ancestry was Hon. Ezra Cornell, the founder of Cornell University, who descended from one, possibly from both, of the brothers above named.

Ezra Cornell was grandson of Reuben Barnard, of Nantucket, and, during a visit to the island some years ago, spent some time in looking through Friends' records there.

RICHARD SWAIN came to the island with his second wife (the widow of George Bunker) and his family. While living at Hampton he was " select-man and *commissioner* for small causes, in 1639 he had liberty to settle small claims." John, the son of his first wife, married Mary, daughter of Nathaniel Wier.†

---

* The favorite motto of St. Bernard was "Sustine et abstine" (bear and forbear); the same motto is found on the Barnard or Bernard coat of arms.

† "Nathaniel Weare, Newbury, son, perhaps, of Peter, of the same, born in England about 1631, . . . became counsellor of N. H. . . . married Elizabeth, daughter of Richard Swain of Rowley." (Savage, vol. iv. p. 441.)

Richard Swain (Rowley, 1639), came to America in the "True-

Richard, the son of his second wife, moved to New Jersey; Richard Swain, Sr., died in 1682, his son John in 1717. This family were members of the Society of Friends.

JOHN SWAIN, the proprietor (son of Richard Swain, Sr.), has left a record in his house, known as the oldest house on the island, which is still standing, although much out of repair.

---

love," 1635, aged thirty-four; settled at Hampton; married, in 1658. Jane Bunker, widow of George. Richard Swain's daughter Elizabeth married Nathaniel Weare.

John Swain, of Nantucket, probably son of Richard Swain the first, married Mary, daughter of Nathaniel Wyer. (Savage, vol. iv. p. 234.)

This must have been a daughter of the first Nathaniel, alluded to below, and a sister of Nathaniel who married Elizabeth Swain, or, if a daughter of the second Nathaniel, the child of a wife previous to Elizabeth.

N. E. Hist. and Gen. Reg., vol. xxv. p. 246, says, "The family of Wier is one of good standing in Scotland whose name is said to be the same as Vere."

"In early years in this country were persons spelling their name Weare, Weir, Weyer, Wier, Wire, Wyer, all probably intending the same name, and many, if not all, possibly belonging to one family."

"First was Robert Wyer of Boston, next Peter Weare who died in Newbury."

"There was a Nathaniel Weare or Wire early in Newbury, afterwards of Nantucket, where he died March 1st, 1681, who had a daughter Hester, wife of Benjamin Swett and Stephen Greenleaf and a son Nathaniel who married in Newbury 3 December 1656 Elizabeth Swain, moved to Hampton, was a Councillor and Chief Justice of New Hampshire, and died 18 May 1718 leaving sons Nathaniel and Peter" and, Savage says, "six others."

PETER FOLGER.

BENJAMIN FRANKLIN, in his genealogical notes, infers
that the Folger family was of Flemish origin, and went
to England in the time of Queen Elizabeth.

Peter Folger, son of John Folger, was born in
1617, and came from Norwich, England, in 1635.

He went with his father to Martha's Vineyard, where
he taught a school and surveyed land; he also assisted
Thomas Mayhew, Jr., in his labors as a missionary
among the Indians.

He was a Baptist, but it is believed that when an old
man he embraced the views of Friends.

Although he was not one of the first proprietors of
Nantucket, he may be regarded as a very early settler,
having removed to the island in 1663.

"Nantucket, 4ᵗʰ July, 1663.

"These presents witnesseth that we whose names
are underwritten do give and grant unto peter foulger,
half a share of accomodations on the land above sayd,
that is to say half so much as one of the twenty purchasers, both in respect of upland, meadow, wood,
timber and other appurtenances belonging to him and
his hiers forever on condition that he com to inhabit
on Ifland aforesayd with his family within one year
after the sale hereof. Likewise that the sayd peter
shall atend the English in the way of an Interpreter
between the Indians and them upon al necessary oca-
sions, his house lot to be layd at the place commonly

called by the name of Rogers field so as may be most convenient.

"Witness our hands.

"John Smyth   "Tristram Coffin Sr
"Thos Macy   for myself and others
"Edward Starbuck   being empowered by
"John Swayne   them.
"Robert Barnard
"Richard Swayne   "Peter Coffin
"John Rolfe   "Steven Greenleaf
"Thos Mayhew   "Tristram Coffin Jr
                     "William Pile for two
                         shares
                     "Nathaniel Starbuck
                     "Thomas Coffin"

Cotton Mather describes Peter Folger as an "Able Godley Englishman who was employed in teaching the youth in Reading, Writing and the Principles of Religion by Catechism, being well learned likewise in the Scriptures and Capable of Help in religious matters."

At Nantucket he was chosen clerk of the court and recorder July 21, 1673; he also surveyed lands for the settlers, and was regarded as the scholar of the community.

The varied employments of Peter Folger prove him to have been as versatile as industrious; to him, at least, "the knowing Folgers lazy" could not have been applied; and if there was ever any foundation in fact for the character which the little Nantucket rhyme has fastened upon this family, it must have been earned by a later representative of the name.

His mantle fell upon some of his descendants, and he bequeathed to them decided ability.

" His son Eleazer and Eleazer, Jr., were intelligent literary and mathematical."

Peter Folger died in 1690; Mary, his widow, in 1704.

Abiah Folger, the youngest child of Peter Folger, and the only one born on Nantucket, married Josiah Franklin, of Boston.

Benjamin Franklin, son of Josiah and Abiah (Folger) Franklin, married Deborah Read, of Philadelphia.

Richard Bache, born in England, in 1737, immigrated to the United States, where he married, in 1767, Sarah, only daughter of Benjamin and Deborah (Read) Franklin. Richard Bache was Postmaster-General of the United States in 1776.

Richard Bache's marriage with Sarah, daughter of Benjamin Franklin, continues the Folger family line in Philadelphia, Mrs. E. D. Gillespie, of Philadelphia, being a grand-daughter of Richard Bache.* This branch of Peter Folger's family has made its mark in many lines of work; there have been among the generations which have succeeded the great philosopher men who have reached distinction in the army and navy, as men of letters, at the bar, and in the service of the church, and women who in patriotic and educational work have proved the ability transmitted to them from their venerable ancestor.

It is gratifying to note in the autobiography of Franklin that he was deeply interested in his ancestors, nor did he consider time lost when in England he made

---

* Other descendants in this line intermarried with Irwin, Hodge, Humphrey, Davis, Pepper, and Perry (of the family of Commodore Perry).

an effort to ascertain from records there the past history of his family.

WALTER FOLGER, another descendant of Peter Folger, was son of Walter and Elizabeth (Starbuck) Folger. Elizabeth was daughter of Thomas Starbuck.

Walter Folger first was son of Barzillai and Phebe (Coleman) Folger.

Barzillai was son of Nathan, who was son of Eleazer and Sarah (Gardner) Folger, and Eleazer was son of Peter Folger.

Walter Folger second practised law for twenty years, and was for six years judge of the Court of Common Pleas, during which time no case decided by him was ever carried to a higher court; he was six years in the Massachusetts Senate, one year in the House of Representatives of Massachusetts, and four years in the Congress of the United States; in addition to this he was one of the best mathematicians and mechanics of his day. He has left as a record of his mechanical skill a remarkable clock, still in the possession of his family.

He commenced work upon this clock at the age of twenty-two, and, devoting to it his leisure hours only, completed it in the course of the second year.

It was put in motion July 4, 1790, and in 1895, though brown with age, it is a good time-keeper; the glass only which covered its face has been renewed. William C. Folger says, "He made not only the works but the case also, I am told."

"It is made of brass and steel. It keeps the date of the year and the day of the month; the sun and moon rise and set in accordance with those in the heavens; it also shows the earth's place on the ecliptic; it keeps the moon's nodes around the ecliptic; the wheel that keeps the date of the year revolves once in one hundred years, remaining still ten years, and at the expiration of each ten years it starts regularly one notch; the diurnal motion of the sun is represented by a circular metallic plate so adjusted that it is seen through a slit in the dial-plate at a greater or less meridian altitude, as the declination changes, rising and setting as in nature, and changing the time in conformity to the latitude, . . . giving also through the entire day the time of his rising and setting and place of the earth on the ecliptic; the moon is represented by a spherule exhibited to the eye in the same manner, but by having one hemisphere colored, and, by a process much more complicated, shows not only the rising, setting, and southing of the moon with the time of full sea at Nantucket, but also the chief phenomena dependent on the obliquity of the moon's path to the ecliptic, such as the hunter's and harvest moons.

"Some of these involve a motion of the works through a period of eighteen years and two hundred and twenty-five days, and the wheel by which the date of the year is advertised is so constructed that its revolution is only completed in one hundred years."

Walter Folger never learned a trade, never studied law with a lawyer, nor went to any institution of learning where anything above the alphabet, spelling, reading in the Bible, arithmetic, and surveying were taught.

MARIA MITCHELL, late Professor of Astronomy at Vassar College, whose mathematical ability needs no comment to the present generation, was a lineal descendant of Peter Folger. Maria Mitchell was daughter of William and Lydia (Coleman) Mitchell. Lydia

Coleman was daughter of Andrew Coleman, who was son of Enoch, who was son of Jeremiah, who was son of John, who married Joanna Folger, daughter of Peter Folger. On the paternal side as well she was descended from Peter Folger, and from many of the early settlers on the Island. (See pages 83–87.)

The connection of the Barker family with Nantucket and with the family of Peter Folger furnishes a link between Nantucket and Plymouth.

JACOB BARKER, financier and merchant, was son of
    Robert Barker and Sarah Gardner.
Robert Barker was son of
    Samuel Barker and Bethiah *Folger*.
Samuel Barker was son of
    Isaac Barker and Judith *Prence*.
Bethiah Folger was daughter of
    John, and grand-daughter of PETER FOLGER.

JUDITH PRENCE was daughter of
    GOVERNOR THOMAS PRENCE and Mary Collier,
      and grand-daughter of
    WILLIAM COLLIER.

WILLIAM COLLIER, whose daughter Mary was second wife of Governor Prence, was a wealthy merchant, who came early to Plymouth and soon removed to Duxbury.* It is not known whether he brought with him a wife, but Savage says " four daughters of excellent character came with him,"—Sarah, who married Love Brewster; Mary, who married Thomas Prence; Elizabeth, who married Constant Southworth; and Rebecca. William Collier was assistant governor twenty-eight

---

* Savage, vol. i. p. 448.

years,* member of Council of War four years,† member
of Provincial Congress in 1643, and one of the committee of two appointed by Congress to sign the Articles
of Confederation.‡   He died in Duxbury in 1671.

THOMAS PRENCE was born at Lechdale, Gloucester-
shire, England, in 1600; he died in Plymouth, Massachusetts, in 1673.   He was governor of the Plymouth
Colony eighteen years, assistant thirteen years, treasurer one year, member of the Council of War five
years, commissioner twelve years, alternate commissioner several years.   The N. E. Hist. and Gen. Reg.,
vol. vi. p. 234, thus speaks of him:

" He was a worthy gentleman and very able for his
office, and faithful in the discharge thereof, studious of
peace, a well willer to all that feared God and a terror
to the wicked."

Doubtless from various records Thomas Prence was
a zealot in his own belief and intolerant of all whose
views did not accord with his; it must be remembered
that in that day intolerance was the rule and charity
the exception.

Governor Prence and his associates believed they
were engaged in their Master's service in any persecutions they were party to, and the author of " The
Pilgrim Republic" says, " A severe execution of the
laws was exceptional with them and they often exer-
cised leniency on slight pretexts."

He further says, " Thomas Prence had ever swayed
the courts in religious matters.   Let it stand as a

---

* Plymouth Colonial Records, vol. i. pp. 82–86, etc.

† Ibid., vol. ii. pp. 47, 64.

‡ See Winsor's History of Duxbury, p. 90, and Savage, vol. i. p.
433.

redeeming trait to his character that he used this influence to emancipate his people from the bonds of a world-wide superstition.* Prence also honored himself by zealously promoting public education. . . . The stern Calvinism which he cherished had long been losing its hold on the public mind and the signs of the times were ominous to those conservative principles which he considered essential to a good government . . . it is probable that the weary Governor was quite ready to go when death summoned him from the Government-house April 8, 1673 at the age of seventy-three.†

"Ten days later with all the ceremony due to his office he was laid on Burial Hill in a grave now unknown."

WILLIAM ALLEN BUTLER belongs to this branch of the family, his great-grandmother having been a half-sister of Jacob Barker and daughter of the aforesaid Robert Barker.

Another descendant of Peter Folger was the late CHARLES JAMES FOLGER, who was born at Nantucket in 1818; when he was thirteen years of age the family removed to Geneva, New York. He graduated at Hobart College in 1836, read law with Mark H. Sibley, and was admitted to the bar in 1839. He was judge, State senator, chief justice, sub-treasurer of the United States, in New York, and finally Secretary of the Treasury of the United States.

---

* Witchcraft.

† For dates and authority concerning the services of Thomas Prence, see Justin Winsor's History of Duxbury ; Plymouth Colony Records ; Savage ; N. E. Hist. and Gen. Reg. ; and The Pilgrim Republic, by John A. Goodwin.

THOMAS GARDINER AND HIS SONS RICHARD AND JOHN GARDNER.

THOMAS GARDINER, or Gardner, the first of the Salem stock, came to America from England, in 1624, where the family had flourished for more than three centuries.

He was chief ruler or governor of the Cape Ann Colony, under the auspices of the Dorchester Company.*

Not realizing here the success intended, he removed to Salem and was elected the same year representative to the General Court; † he was member of the Town Council of Salem for a number of years. ‡

From Historical Collections of Essex Institute of Salem, we learn that the name of Gardner has been known and respected throughout the entire history of the city.

Thomas Gardiner had several sons, among whom, as early settlers of Nantucket, although not original proprietors, were Richard and John, who took an active part in affairs civil and military.

Austin says that Richard Gardner lived at Salem from 1648 to 1666; he and his wife (Sarah Shattuck) were persecuted for attending Quaker Meeting, and went to Nantucket, where they spent the remainder of their lives.

In 1673, Governor Lovelace commissioned Richard

---

* N. E. Hist. and Gen. Reg., vol. xxv. pp. 48, 49.

† Mass. Col. Records, vol. i. p. 204.

‡ One Hundred and Sixty Allied Families.

Note.—Some descendants of Lion Gardiner live now on Nantucket; whether there is any connection between Governor Gardiner and Lion Gardiner is not known.

as chief magistrate of Nantucket, "he to hold his commission until the next election and return and approbation of a new one by Francis Lovelace." *

Copy of "A Letter from the Secretary to yᵉ Inhabᵗˢ of Nantuckett. [Deeds III. 89, Secretary's Office.]

"New Yorke, Apr. yᵉ 24th, 1673.

"Gent:—By the Governoᵣ Ordᵣ I am to acquaint you, That hee Received your Letter (bearing Date the 3d Day of Aprill) about three weeks fince, by the Hands of Mr. Richard Gardner, together with eight Barrels of ffifh for two Yeares, Acknowledgement, and a Token of fifty weight of ffeathers, for which your Care of the Former and Kindnefs in the Latter hee Returns you Thanks. There came to the Governoᵣ in the Winter a Letter from Mr Tristram Coffin about your Election, but no other from you; in anfwer to which you had heard from him fooner, but the Difficulty of Conveyance hindered. You will now underftand the Governors Choice, by the Bearers hereof Mr. Richard and Captain John Gardner;

"That is, Mr. Richard Gardner for Chiefe Magiftrate this Yeare, and Capt. John Gardner for Chiefe Military Officer, for which they have Commiffions. They have alfo with them fome Additional Inftructions and Directions to Communicate to you; moft of which were Propofed by thofe two ffriends you sent who have prudently Managed the Truft you Repofed in them. They have alfo with them a Booke of the Lawes of the Government, and three Conftables Staves;

---

* Authority for this commission may be found on pp. 87, 88, in a manuscript volume entitled Deeds, Vol. 3, in the office of the Secretary of State in Albany.

" As to your Non-performance of the Acknowledgement according to the Strictnefs of the Time, his Hono' being fenfible that Opportunityes doe not very frequently prefent between these Places, hee is very well Satisfyed with your Civill Excufe. If at any Time you have other Propofalls to make, for the Good of yo' Inhabitants, you may reft affured of his Hono' ready Complyance therein. This is all I have in Charge to Deliver unto you from the Governour, foe take Leave and Subscribe

" Gent: Yo' very humble Servant
" MATTHIAS NICOLLS."

JOHN GARDNER was magistrate at Nantucket in 1680, and judge of probate from 1699 until his death, which occurred in 1706, at the age of eighty-two. He is referred to by Cotton Mather as being " well acquainted with the Indians, having divers years assisted them in their government, by instructing them in the laws of England and deciding difficult cases among them.* In 1673, John Gardner was appointed " Captain and Chief Military Officer of the Ffoot Company."

Copy of " Commiffion for Cap' John Gardner of the Ifland of Nantucket, to bee Capt. of the Foot Company there. [Deeds III. 88, Secretary's Office.]

" Francis Lovelace, Esq'., &c: Governo' Gen'll under his Royall H' James Duke of Yorke and Albany, &c;

---

* From no records do we read of serious difficulties *on Nantucket* between the Indians and the white men, they followed the example of the settlers in fishing for whales, which were plentiful on that shoal-bound coast, and " becamo the most expert of the original whalers of Nantucket." This industry was first carried on in small open boats at short distances from shore.

of all his Territoryes in America; To Cap[t]. John Gardner of y[e] Island Nantuckett. Whereas, You are one of the two Persons returned unto mee by the Inhab[ts] of your Ifland, to bee the Chiefe Military Officer there, having conceived a good opinion of your ffittnefs and Capacity; By Vertue of the Commiffion and Authority unto mee given by his Royall Highneffe, James Duke of Yorke and Albany, I have Constituted and Appointed, and by these Presents doe hereby Constitute and Appoint you John Gardner to be Captaine and Chiefe Military Officer of the ffoot Company rifsen or to bee rifen within the Iflands of Nantuckett and Tuckanuckett; you are to take the said Company into your Charge and Care as Captaine thereof, and them duly to Exercise in Armes; and all Officers and Souldyers belonging to the said Company are to Obey you as their Captaine.

" And you are to follow fuch Orders and Inftructions, as you fhall from Time to Time Receive from mee or other your Superiour Officers according to the discipline of Warr; for the doeing whereof this fhall be your Comiffion.

Note.—John Gardner's daughter Rachel married John Brown, of Salem, son of Elder John Brown and Hannah (Hobart).

Hannah Hobart was daughter of Rev. Peter Hobart, who was born in Hingham, County of Norfolk, England, in 1604, and died in Hingham, Massachusetts, January 20, 1679. (Hobart Family Memorial, Part I., pp. 103, 104, No. 23., III. A.)

He was the first minister of the Gospel in Hingham, Massachusetts, was educated at Cambridge, England, and came to New England June 8, 1635; was admitted freeman same year, and settled at Hingham in September, 1635.

Savage, vol. ii. p. 435, says he took his A.B. in 1625, his A.M. in 1629, that he wrote his name Hubberd, was of the Magdalen College, and had preached at divers places, last at Haverhill, in Suffolk, before coming here.

" Given under my Hand and Seale at Fort James in New Yorke this 15th Day of Aprill in the 25th Yeare of his Maties Reigne, Annoq° Domini, 1673.

"FRAN. LOVELACE."

Savage further says,—

" Peter brought with him a wife and four children certainly,—viz.:

" Joshua Hobart.

" Jeremiah Hobart.

" Josiah Hobart.

" Elizabeth Hobart, *m.* John Ripley.

" And after coming here thirteen were added to the number,—viz.:

" Icabod Hobart.

" Hannah Hobart, died soon.

" Hannah Hobart, *m.* John Brown, of Salem.

" Bathsheba Hobart, *m.* Joseph Turner, of Scituate, 1640.

" Israel Hobart, *m.* Sarah Wetherill, dau. of Rev. William Wetherill, 1668.

" Jael Hobart, *m.* Joseph Bradford, son of Governor Bradford.

" Gershom Hobart, *m.* Sarah ——.

" Japhet Hobart, *m.*

" Nehemiah Hobart, *m.* Sarah Jackson, 1678.

" David Hobart, *m.* 1st, Joanna Quincy, dau. Edmund Quincy second ; 2d, Sarah Joyce.

" Rebecca Hobart, *m.* Daniel Mason, of Stonington (as second wife).

" Abigail Hobart, *unm.*

" Lydia Hobart, *m.* Captain Thomas Lincoln, 1690 (as second wife), and [Savage adds] ' the patriarch died 1679.'

" In Rev. Peter Hobart's will, made four days before his death, he names fourteen living children, and wife Rebecca (probably daughter of Richard Ibrook), who was mother of the last six children ; no mention is made in Hingham records of the death of the first wife.

" Edmund Hobart, father of Rev. Peter Hobart, was a member of the General Court, 1639–40–42, from Hingham, Massachusetts. He brought a wife and several children with him from England in 1635, and died in 1646, leaving Edmund, Joshua, Rev. Peter, Thomas, and two daughters, Rebecca and Sarah."

SAMUEL SHATTUCK.

THE name of SAMUEL SHATTUCK is associated with
Nantucket through the marriage of his daughter,
Sarah Shattuck,* to Richard Gardner; by this mar-
riage Samuel Shattuck became the ancestor of many
Nantucket people.

Samuel Shattuck, who is described as " an inhabitant of Salem of good repute," was born in England
about 1620; on coming to this country he settled in
Salem, Massachusetts.

A stone still standing over his grave in Salem bears
the following inscription:

"Here lyeth buried y⁰ body of Samuel Shattuck
aged 69 years who departed this life in y⁰ 6th day of
June 1689." He was present at a Friend's Meeting
when Christopher Holder attempted to speak, and he
"endeavored to prevent their thrusting a handkerchief
into Holder's mouth lest it should have choked him,"
for which attempt he was carried to Boston and imprisoned till he had "given bond to answer it at the
next Court and not to come to any Quaker meeting."

The following extracts are taken from the edition of
Besse's " Collection of The Sufferings of the People
called Quakers," printed in London in 1753 (vol. ii. pp.
187, 188.)

---

* It has been the belief of many descendants of Sarah (Shattuck)
Gardner that she was a daughter of Samuel Shattuck, and Savage
(vol. ii. p. 229) says, "Richard Gardner married Sarah Shattuck,
probably daughter of Samuel;" other authorities give Samuel with
Sarah in a list of the children of Damaris Shattuck (widow who married Thomas Gardiner).

A Letter of the Prisoners to the Magistrates at the Court in Salem.

"Friends:

"Whereas it was your Pleasures to commit us, whose names are underwritten, to the House of Correction in Boston, although the Lord the righteous Judge of Heaven and Earth is our witness, that we had done nothing worthy of Stripes or of Bonds, and we being committed by your Court to be dealt withal as the Law provides for foreign Quakers, as y* please to term us; and having some of us suffered your Law and Pleasures, now that which we do expect is, now to be set free by the same Law, as your Manner is with Strangers and not to put us in upon the Account of one Law and execute another Law upon us, of which, according to your own Manner, we were never convicted as the Law expresses. If you had sent us upon the Account of your new Law, we should have expected the Gaoler's Order to have been on that Account, which that it was not, appears by the Warrant which we have, and the Punishment which we bare, as four of us were whipped, among whom was one that had formerly been whipt, so now also, according to your former Law. Friends, let it not be a small Thing in your Eyes, the exposing, as much as in you lies, our families to Ruin.

"It's not unknown to you, the Season, and the Time of the Year, for those that live of Husbandry, and what their Cattle and Families may be exposed unto; and also such as live on Trade.

"We know if the Spirit of Christ did dwell and rule in you, these Things would take Impression upon your Spirits.

"What our Lives and Conversations have been, in
that place is well known, and what we now suffer for,
is much for false Reports and ungrounded Jealousies of
Heresy and Sedition. These Things lie upon us to lay
before you. As for our Parts, we have true Peace and
Rest in the Lord in all our Sufferings, and are made
willing in the Power and Strength of God, freely to
offer up our Lives in this Cause of God, for which we
suffer; Yea, and we do find, through Grace, the En-
largements of God in our imprisoned Estate, to whom
alone we commit ourselves and Families, for the dis-
posing of us according to his infinite Wisdom and
Pleasure, in whose Love is our Rest and Life.

"From the House of Bondage in Boston, wherein
we are made captives, by the Wills of Men, although
made free by the Son of God, John VIII—36. In
which we quietly rest this 16th of the Fifth month 1658.

"LAURENCE.
"CASSANDRA. } SOUTHWICK.
"JOSIAH.
"SAMUEL SHATTUCK.
"JOSHUA BUFFUM."

"On the 11th of the Third Month, 1659, the aforesaid Laurence and Cassandra Southwick, their son
Josiah, Samuel Shattuck, and others were called before
the Court, and as they continued steadfast in what
the governor was pleased to call rebellion against
the Authority of the country the Sentence of Banishment was pronounced against them, and but a Fort-
night's Time allowed for them to depart, on pain of
Death, nor would they grant them any longer Time,
though desired: So the said Samuel Shattuck, Nicholas Phelps, and Josiah Southwick were obliged to

take an Opportunity that presented four Days after
to pass for England by Barbadoes. The aged couple
Laurence and Cassandra went to Shelter Island where
shortly after they died within three Days of each other;
and Joshua Buffum departed to Rhode Island." (Vol.
II., page 198.)

Copy of the King's Letter or Mandamus.

"Trusty and Wellbeloved, we greet you well.
Having been informed that several of our Subjects
among you, called Quakers, have been and are imprisoned by you, whereof some have been executed,
and others (as hath been represented unto us) are in
Danger to undergo the Like: We have thought fit to
signify our Pleasure, in that Behalf for the future, and
do require, that if there be any of those People called
Quakers amongst you, now already condemned to suffer
Death, or other Corporal Punishment, or that are imprisoned, or obnoxious to the like Condemnation, you
are to forbear to proceed any farther, but that you
forthwith send the said Persons (whether condemned
or imprisoned) over to this our Kingdom of England,
together with their respective Crimes or Offences laid
to their Charge, to the End such Course may be taken
with them here, as shall be agreeable to our Laws and
their Demerits. And for so doing, these our Letters
shall be your sufficient Warrant and Discharge. Given
at our Court at Whitehall the 9th Day of September
1661 in the thirteenth year of our Reign."

"Subscribed, To our Trusty and Welbeloved John
Endicot Esq. and to all and every other the Governour
or Governours of our Plantation of New England, and
of the Colonies thereunto belonging, that now are or

hereafter shall be; And to all and every the Minister's and Officers of our said Plantation and Colonies whatever within the Continent of New England.

"By His Majesty's Command.

"WIL. MORRIS."

(Vol. II., Page 225.)

"In procuring the aforesaid Letter or Mandamus from the King, Edward Burroughs was a principle Instrument for when the News of W. Leddra's Death came to the Ears of the Friends at London, and of the Danger many others of their Persuasion were in, they were much concerned, especially the said Edward Burroughs, who speedily repaired to the Court and having got Access to the King's Presence, told him, *There was a Vein of innocent Blood opened in his Dominions, which if it were not stopped might overrun all.* To which the King replied, *But I will stop that Vein.* Then Burroughs desired him to do it speedily, for there was Danger of many others being soon put to Death.

"The King answered, *As speedy as you will* and ordered the Secretary to be called, and the Mandamus to be forthwith granted.

"A few Days after Edward Burroughs went again to the King, desiring Dispatch of the Business. The King said, He had no present Occasion to send a Ship thither, but if they would send one, they might as soon as they would.

"The King also granted his Deputation to Samuel Shattock who had been banished thence, to carry his Mandamus to New England.

"Whereupon an Agreement was made with Ralph Goldsmith, one of the said People called Quakers, and Master of a good Ship, for 300*l* to sail forthwith.

"He immediately prepared for his Voyage and in about six weeks arrived in Boston Harbor, on a First-day of the Week.

"The Townsmen seeing a Ship with English Colours soon came on board and asked for the Captain.

"Ralph Goldsmith told them he was the Commander. They asked, Whether he had any Letters? He answered, *Yes.* But withal told them, *He would not deliver them that Day.*

"So they returned on shore again, and reported, that There were many Quakers come, and that Samuel Shattuck (who they knew had been banished on pain of Death) was among them.

"But they knew nothing of his Errand or Authority.

"Thus all was kept close, and none of the Ship's Company suffered to go on shore that Day.

"Next morning Ralph Goldsmith the Commander, with Samuel Shattuck, the King's Deputy, went on shore, and sending the Boat back to the Ship, they two went directly through the Town to the Governour's House, and knockt at the Door: He sending a Man to know their Business, they sent him Word, that their Message was from the King of England, and that they would deliver it to none but himself.

"Then they were admitted to go in, and the Governour came to them and commanded Samuel Shattuck's Hat to be taken off, and having received the Deputation and the Mandamus, he laid off his own Hat, and ordering Shattuck's Hat to be given him again, perused the Papers, and then went out to the Deputy-Governour's, bidding the King's Deputy and the Master of the Ship to follow him : Being come to the Deputy-Governour's and having consulted him, he

5

returned to the aforesaid two Persons, and said, We shall obey his Majesty's Command.

"After this the Master of the Ship gave Liberty to his Passengers to come on shore, which they did and had a religious Meeting with their Friends of the Town, where they returned Praises to God for his Mercy manifested in this wonderful Deliverance.

"Not long after the following order at Boston was issued:

"To WILLIAM SALTER Keeper of the Prison at Boston.

"You are required, by Authority and Order of the General-Court forthwith to release and discharge the Quakers who at present are in your Custody: See that you dont neglect this.

"By Order of the Court
"EDWARD RAWSON, *Secretary.*

"BOSTON the 9th of
December 1661."

To the instrumentality of Samuel Shattuck, aided by Edward Burroughs, is due the discontinuance, for a time at least, of one of the most iniquitous persecutions ever carried on, instigated by those who themselves had suffered for conscience' sake. Whipping and imprisonment were later resorted to, but never to the same extent.

With this mandate from the king, Samuel Shattuck was safe to live thereafter a peaceable life in Salem.

The usual character accorded to the early settlers of New England for extraordinary Christian names is exemplified by a son Retire and a daughter Return, mentioned in records of Samuel Shattuck. These were supposed to be commemorative of his banishment and return.

These two children probably died young, as in the division of the property they are not mentioned; at all events the names have not descended.

Note.—In Besse's History is an account of the death of William Robinson, Marmaduke Stephenson, William Leddra, and Mary Dyer, who suffered martyrdom by hanging in Boston in 1660 for their firm adherence to the principles of truth as professed by Friends. Wenlock Christisen was under sentence of death when Samuel Shattuck returned from England bearing the mandamus from King Charles Second requiring the release of all Friends from prison.

THOMAS MAYHEW AND THOMAS MAYHEW, Jr.

That THOMAS MAYHEW was a proprietor of Nantucket has been previously shown. He selected "his sonne" Thomas Mayhew, Jr., as his associate.

It is probable that Thomas Mayhew, Sr., never had more than a business connection with Nantucket, but one of his descendants married a descendant of Peter Folger.

Thomas Mayhew was born early in 1592, and was a merchant of Southampton, England, but emigrated to America in 1633 or 1634, was admitted a freeman May 14, 1634, and early in 1635 settled at Watertown, Massachusetts, where he owned mills purchased of Mr. Cradock, and a farm; he was at one time proprietor of the Oldham farm. He was a selectman from 1637 to 1643, and a representative to the General Court from 1636 to 1644.

In 1641 he obtained a grant of Martha's Vineyard, and sent there his son Thomas and several other persons who settled at Edgartown. (History of Watertown.) He himself did not move to Martha's Vineyard until 1644 or 1645.

Whether he brought any other children from England has not been ascertained.

Cotton Mather says of him,—

"The worshipful Thomas Mayhew in the year 1641 obtained a grant of Martha's Vineyard, Nantucket and Elizabeth Isles to make a settlement.

Note.—William C. Folger's MS. says, "The first Mayhew known in England was Simon, who went there in 1000 A.D. from Normandy, settled in County of Wiltshire, and from Wiltshire came Thomas Mayhew to America."

"His son Mr Thomas Mayhew in the year 1642 settl'd at Martha's Vineyard with a few other Inhabitants where his Reputation for Piety, his Natural Gifts, besides the acquir'd by his Education (having attained no small knowledge in the Latin and Greek tongues; and being not wholly a stranger to the Hebrew) soon occasioned his Call to the Ministry among that handful.

"In 1647 he intended a short voyage for England, but alas, the ship wherein he took passage was never heard of."

Of Thomas Mayhew, the governor, he says,—

"I have already told my Reader that the Government of this People was the best (of all Governments) Monarchy; and it has been Judged not without Reason, that a main Obstruction in the Progress of the Gospel in the American Plantation, was, if not yet is, the Jealousie the Princes conceiv'd of the Invasion of their Government through the Pretences of Religion and the Eclipsing their Monarchical Dignity.

"Mr Thomas Mayhew therefore finding that the Princes on these Islands, who although they maintained their Absolute Power and Jurisdiction as Kings, were yet bound to do certain Homage to a Potent Prince on the Continent; and although they were no great People, yet had been wasted in Indian Wars, wherein the Great Princes on the Continent (not unlike European Princes for like Reasons of State) were not unassisting, whereby they were necessitated to make these Princes the Balance to decide their Controversies, and several Jurisdictions, by Presents annually sent, whereby obliging the Princes to give their several Assistance as Occasion requir'd.

"And seeing his son, as aforesaid, in a Zealous Endeavor for their Conversion he judged it meet that Moses and Aaron joyn Hands.

"He therefore prudently lets them know, that by Order from his Master the King of England, he was to govern the English which should inhabit these Islands;

"That his Master was in Power far above any of the Indian Monarchs; but that as he was Powerful so was he a great Lover of Justice:

"That therefore he would in no measure invade their Jurisdiction but on the Contrary assist them as Need required:

"That Religion and Government were distinct Things.

"Thus in no long time they conceiv'd no ill Opinion of the Christian Religion." (B VI., Magnalia Section III.)

In closing the history of Thomas Mayhew's Government he says,—

"I shall close the whole when I have told the Reader that their Children are generally taught to Read and Write.

"In one of their towns last winter viz: 1693, thirty Children were at school, twenty more of the same place, accidentally, being not supplied with books could not attend to it.

"Such who are too far distant from any school are often taught by some of their neighbors; in divers places there are lesser schools."

Thomas Mayhew, Jr., left three sons (who subsequently assumed a leading part in the affairs of these islands.) These sons were named Thomas, John, and Matthew.

To his grandchildren Thomas Mayhew alludes in

a postscript of a letter to Governor Edmond Andros : *

" May it please yo' Hono' to image what I have on
these Islands

Graund Sonnes 15
My sonnes sonnes sonnes 8
Daughters 8
Graund Daughters 11
                                              ――
                                              82

" I prayfe God two of my Graund-sons doe preach
to English and Indians, Matthew sometimes to the
younge."

Thomas, the grandson, died in 1715, and John in
1689, aged thirty-seven years.

Experience Mayhew, a minister, author of " Indian
Converts or Some Account of the Lives and Dyeing
Speeches of Christianized Indians of Martha's Vineyard in New England," published in London 1727,
was a son of John Mayhew.

Jonathan Mayhew, who was born in Martha's Vineyard, October 8, 1720, and died in Boston, July 9,
1766, was a clergyman and an advocate of liberalism ;
he was a son of Experience Mayhew.

---

* N. Y. Col. MSS., xxiv., Secretary's Office.

EXTRACTS FROM JOURNALS OF JOHN RICHARDSON AND THOMAS STORY, GIVING SOME ACCOUNT OF THE RISE OF FRIENDS ON NANTUCKET.

JOHN RICHARDSON says, "It was much with me, when on Rhode Island to visit Nantucket, where there were but very few Friends. . . .

"We landed safe, and as we went up an Ascent we saw a great many people looking towards the Sea, for great Fear had possess'd them, that our Sloop was a French Sloop loaded with Men and Arms, who were coming to invade the Island; I held out my Arms and told them, I knew not of any worse Arms than these on board.

"They said, they were glad it was no worse, for they had intended to have alarmed the Island, it being a time of war. I told the good-like People, for so they appear'd to me, That Peleg Slocum near Rhode Island, was Master of the Sloop, and that we came to visit them in the Love of God, if they would be willing to let us have some Meetings, amongst them. They behaved themselves very courteously towards us and said, They thought we might.

"We then enquired for Nathaniel Starbuck, who we understood was in some degree convinced of the Truth, and having Directions to his House, we went thither and I told him, We made bold to come to his House, and if he was free to receive us we would stay a little with him, but if not, we would go elsewhere; for we heard he was a seeking religious Man and such chiefly we were come to visit;

"He said, We were very welcome. And by this Time came in his Mother Mary Starbuck who the Islanders esteemed as a Judge among them for little of Moment was done there without her, as I understood.

" At the first Sight of her it sprang in my Heart, To this Woman is the everlasting Love of God. I looked upon her as a Woman that bore some Sway in the Island, and so I said and that truly, We are come in the Love of God to visit you, if you are willing to let us have some Meetings among you : She said, She thought we might. . . .

" The next Consideration was Where shall this meeting be ? She paused awhile and then said, I think at our House.

" I from thence gathered she had an Husband, for I thought the Word *our* carried in it some Power besides her own, and I presently found he was with us : " I then made my Observation on him, and he appeared not a Man of mean Parts, but she so far exceeded him in Soundness of Judgment, Clearness of Understanding and an elegant Way of expressing herself, and that not in an affected Strain, but very natural to her, that it tended to lessen the Qualifications of her Husband.

" The Meeting being agreed on and Care taken as to the Appointment of it, we parted, and I lay down to try if I could get any Sleep, . . . but Sleep vanished away from me, and I got up and walked to and fro in the Woods until the Meeting was mostly gathered. I was under a very great Load in my Spirit, but the Occasion of it was hid from me, but I saw it my Place to go to Meeting, the Order of which was such, in all the Parts thereof, I had not seen the like before ; the large and bright rubbed Room was set with suitable Seats or Chairs, the Glass Windows taken out of the Frames and many Chairs placed without very conveniently, so, that I did not see anything awanting, according to the Place, but something to stand on, for I was not free to set my Feet upon the fine Cane Chair, lest I should break it.

"I am the more particular in this exact and exemplary Order than in some other things, for the Seats both within and without Doors, were so placed that the Faces of the People were towards the Seats where the publick Friends sat, and when so set, they did not look or gaze in our Faces, as some I think are too apt to do, which in my Thoughts bespeaks an unconcerned Mind. The Meeting being thus gathered and Set down in this orderly and ample manner (although there were but very few bearing our Name in it) it was not long before the Mighty Power of the Lord began to work, and in it my Companion * especially did appear in Testimony in the fore Part thereof. . . . I sat a considerable Time in the Meeting before I could see my Way clear to say anything, until the Lord's heavenly Power raised me and set me upon my Feet as if one had lifted me up, and what I had first in Commission to speak was in the words of Christ to Nicodemus, viz: Except a Man be born again, he cannot see the Kingdom of God : . . .

"As I was thus opened, and delivering these Things with much more than I can remember, the great Woman I felt for most of an Hour together, fought and strove against the Testimony, sometimes looking up in my Face with a pale and then with a more ruddy Complexion; but the Strength of the Truth increased, and the Lord's mighty Power began to shake the People within and without Doors; but she who was looked upon as a Deborah by these People, was loth

---

* James Bates, who was born in Virginia.

to lose her outside Religion, or the Appearance thereof;
When she could no longer contain, she submitted to
the Power of Truth, and the Doctrines thereof, and
lifted up her Voyce and wept.

"Oh! then the universal Cry and Brokenness of
Heart and Tears was wonderful! From this Time I do
not remember one Word that I spoke in Testimony,
it was enough that I could keep upon the true Bottom, and not be carried away with the Stream above
my Measure. . . . I remember Peleg Slocum (before
mentioned) said after this Meeting, that the like he
was never at, for he thought the Inhabitants of the
Island were shaken, and most of the People convinced
of the Truth. However a great Convincement there
was that Day, Mary Starbuck was one of the Number,
and in a short Time after received a publick Testimony, as did also her son Nathaniel."

It would appear from a journal of Thomas Story,
who was at Nantucket three years later, in 1704, that
there was no settled meeting of Friends until sometime after his visit, wherein he felt it required of him
to lay his concern before Mary Starbuck as the "instrument to bring it about."

Friends' Records of Nantucket Monthly Meeting
state that it was established in 1708.

Thomas Story says, "Before I proceed I think
proper just to give a general Relation of the State of
the People on the Island of Nantucket with respect to
Religion at this Time. This small Island lies about
20 Leagues from the main Land of New England, in-
habited by a mixed People of Various Nations and
some among them called christianized Indians, but
no settled Teachers of any Kind. . . .

"There was in this Island one Nathaniel Starbuck,

whose Wife was a wise discreet Woman, well read in the Scriptures, and not attached unto any Sect, but in great Reputation throughout the Island for her Knowledge in Matters of Religion, and an Oracle among them on that Account, insomuch that they would not do any Thing without her Advice and Content therein;"

It would appear that several ministers of other religious denominations had visited the island from time to time, and had desired a settled maintenance there. This was opposed by Mary Starbuck as "being contrary to the practice of the Apostles and Primitives and the Nature of the Maintenance of a Gospel Ministry, but she would consent so far, as that when any Preacher came among them, that they liked and staid some Time, and took Pains among them, every Family might give unto such what they pleased for the Help of themselves and their Families, if they had any, as Indian Corn (Maze) or other grain, Meal, Flesh, Fish or such other Provisions as they happened to have at the Time to spare, and Wool &c for Cloathing, but nothing certain or settled: For Ministers of Christ ought to travel abroad in the World in that Calling, and not to sit down in one place, unless they have Families to take care of and cannot leave them.

"And Some Time before this John Kinsey, one of our Ministers from Philadelphia, had been to visit them with good Acceptance and had good Service for Truth among them, and had been instrumental in the Hand of the Lord to beget a good liking in them to the Way of Truth, but received nothing from any of them, (for that is not our Way) on account of His Ministry; And I finding a like Concern at this Time and accompanied by Several Friends of both Sexes, we

on the 13th Day of the Fifth Month,* about the tenth
Hour in the Morning, set Sail for the said Island in a
Shallop belonging to our Friend Peleg Slocum, before
mentioned, which under divine Providence, he himself
chiefly conducted, and landed there the next Morning
about six.

"At our landing we went up to the House of the
Widow Mary Gardner where, after some Refreshment
had, came to us Nathaniel Starbuck (Husband of Mary
Starbuck before mentioned) and his son of the same
name, and we proposed to them to have a Meeting
that Day, but there being a court to sit then by Special
Commission, . . . we found it improper at that Time,
and some of our Company went Home with Nathaniel
Starbuck, the elder, and others with his Son, where
we were kindly entertained, tho' Strangers, and they
at that Time, not in the Profession of Truth with us.

"On the 15th we had a Meeting at the House of
Nathaniel Starbuck, the elder, which was pretty large
and open, several of the People being tendered and
generally satisfied with what they heard and felt of
the Goodness and Mercy of God.

"On the 16th being the First Day of the Week, we
had another Meeting there, which was not so large as
was expected, by reason of two Priests, an elderly Man
and a young one, the first from the Isle of Showles,
and the other from Martha's Vineyard, who had a
Meeting near us, the former being come to try if he
could obtain a settled Maintenance among that
People.

"And several being curious to hear this new
Preacher in the Presbyterian Way, it made our Meet-

* 1704.

ing something less than otherwise it might have been, yet it was considerably large, very open and encouraging, for the good Presence of the Lord was with us."

"Many of the Inhabitants of this Island are convinced of the Truth of some Points of the Doctrine of Truth, and some of them have been reached by the divine Virtue and Power of it, but some other Things they do not yet see, and, if there were no Cross, would, in all Appearance, come generally under our Profession; some few are for a Priest and to allow him some Maintenance (for they walk not by Faith but Sight), but the Majority is against it. So that one of these not being able to effect his Purpose went Home in a few Days, but the other staid a little longer. . . .

"This evening we ascended toward the upper Part of the Island to John Swains (one who came to our Meetings and there was only one more, that is Stephen Hussie, in all that Island under our name)."

*   *   *   *   *   *   *

"But one night before we returned from this Island my sleep was taken from me under a concern of mind for the Settlement of a Meeting there; (And though there were two Men under the Profession of Truth among them . . . the chief Instrument pointed to in my Thoughts, by the Truth, for this Service, when we should be gone was Mary Starbuck, before mentioned, to whom I made it known, and in the Opening and Mind of Truth laid a Charge upon her to endeavor to have a Meeting established in their Family once a week at least, to wait upon the Lord with all who were convinced of Truth in the Neighborhood, and in the Island as they had Conveniency.

"This she received with Christian Gravity and it affected her much and became her Concern.

"Having first mentioned it to the Friends who were with me I proposed it likewise to her Children (her Husband being freely passive only in such Things, and naturally good temper'd) who were all discreet young Men and Women, most of them married and hopeful; being all convinced of Truth, they were ready to embrace the Proposal.

"Then I advised them to wait sincerely upon the Lord in such Meetings (for they had no instrumental Teachers) and assured them that I had a firm Confidence in the Lord that he would visit them by his Holy Spirit in them, in his own Time, if they were faithful, held on and did not faint or look back.

"And accordingly, some time after we departed the Island, they did meet, and the Lord did visit them and gathered many unto himself, and they became a large and living Meeting in Him and several living and able Ministers were raised by the Lord in that Family, and of others, to the Honour of His own Arm, who is worthy forever."

For many years the Society prospered, and its large meeting-houses were well filled.

The experience of Nantucket has been a repetition of the history of the Society of Friends in many localities; other religious denominations have attracted the younger people, and the older members, one by one, have passed from works to rewards until a handful only remains of the once flourishing Society of Friends upon Nantucket. Of late, monthly meetings have been held alternately at Nantucket, Lynn, Providence, and Centreville.

In 1894 one meeting-house on the island was sold, and is at present the property of the Historical Society.

AN IMPARTIAL JUDGMENT.

A PENNSYLVANIAN writing of Nantucket one hundred years after the settlement, having visited the island for the purpose of studying its manners and customs, says,—

". . . Here we have none but those which administer to the useful, to the necessary and to the indispensable comforts of life . . . The inhabitants abhor the very idea of expending in useless waste and vain luxuries the fruits of prosperous labor. . . . At home the tender minds of the children must be early struck with the gravity, the serious, though cheerful deportment of their parents; they are inured to a principle of subordination arising neither from sudden passions nor inconsistant pleasure. They are corrected with tenderness, nursed with most affectionate care, clad with that decent plainness from which they observe their parents never to depart; in short by the force of example, more than by precept, they learn to follow the steps of their parents and to despise ostentatiousness as being sinful. They acquire a taste for that neatness for which their fathers are so conspicuous; they learn to be prudent and saving; the very tone of voice in which they are addressed establishes them in that softness of diction which ever after becomes habitual. If they are left with fortunes, they know how to save them, and how to enjoy them with moderation and decency; if they have none they know how to venture; how to work and toil as their parents have done before them . . . As the sea excursions are often very long, the wives are necessarily obliged to transact business, to settle accounts, and, in short, to rule and provide for their families. These circumstances being oft repeated give women the ability, as well as the taste for that kind of superintendency to which, by their prudence and good management, they seem to be in general very equal. This ripens their judgment and justly entitles them to a rank superior to other wives. To this dexterity in managing their husband's business whilst he is absent, the Nantucket women unite a great deal of industry. They spin or cause to be spun, abundance of wool and flax, and would be forever disgraced and looked upon as idlers, if all the family were not clad in good, neat and sufficient homespun cloth. First days are the only seasons when it is lawful for both sexes to exhibit garments of English manufacture, and even these are of the most moderate price and of the gravest colors."

This being the judgment of an outsider surely was impartial, and all of Nantucket descent will be willing to accept the views of a writer so flattering, especially as we have no means of judging of those times excepting by tradition.

Nearly one hundred and fifty added years have wrought many changes, and still we find a justifiable pride in all who claim descent from Mary Starbuck and her contemporaries.

If "the evil that men do lives after them," the lives of the early settlers must have been exceptionally exemplary; there seems to be little recorded discreditable to any of them.

Necessity made them what they were; there could be no idle hands among them; they must work or they must starve; and, at a very early date, the peace of a Quaker influence spread over them proportionate to that of Colonial Philadelphia, and to-day may be heard even among those who belong to the so-called "world's people" "the Thee and the Thou of the Quaker."

DETAIL OF DESCENT FROM PROPRIETORS AND SETTLERS.

MITCHELL FAMILY.

RICHARD MITCHELL, the first of the name of whom we have any record, lived at Bricktown, Isle of Wight, and married Mary Wood.

His son Richard, born in 1686, came to Rhode Island in 1708 and married Elizabeth Tripp; he died in 1722.

One of his descendants says of him, "The firmness with which Richard Mitchell adhered to the religious faith he early adopted, the honesty and integrity that were maintained in all his transactions, the tender, thoughtful care for the welfare of his wife and young family, are striking traits which are inherited by many of his descendants.

". . . He was blessed with a good understanding and sound judgment, and was capable of assisting and advising in matters of difficulty."

Richard, of the next generation, married Mary Starbuck.

Peleg Mitchell, Sr., married Lydia Cartwright.

PELEG MITCHELL, SR., was son of
　Richard Mitchell and Mary *Starbuck*.
Richard Mitchell was son of
　Richard Mitchell and Elizabeth Tripp.
Richard Mitchell was son of
　Richard Mitchell and Mary Wood.

Note.—Names in italics indicate that the ancestor so designated descends from one or more of the "Early Settlers," and that the detail of her ascent to said settler will in its turn be given.

MARY STARBUCK was daughter of
  Jethro Starbuck and Dorcas *Gayer*.
Jethro Starbuck was son of
  Nathaniel Starbuck and Mary *Coffin*.
Nathaniel Starbuck was son of
  EDWARD STARBUCK and Katharine Reynolds.

DORCAS GAYER was daughter of
  William Gayer and Dorcas *Starbuck*.
Dorcas Starbuck was daughter of
  EDWARD STARBUCK and Katharine Reynolds.

MARY COFFIN was daughter of
  TRISTRAM COFFIN and Dionis Stevens.

LYDIA CARTWRIGHT was daughter of
  James Cartwright and Love *Macy*.
James Cartwright was son of
  Hezidiah Cartwright and Abigail Brown.
Hezidiah Cartwright was son of
  Sampson Cartwright and Bethiah *Pratt*.

LOVE MACY was daughter of
  Francis Macy and Judith *Coffin*.
Francis Macy was son of
  Thomas Macy and Deborah *Coffin*.
Thomas Macy was son of
  John Macy and Deborah *Gardner*.
John Macy was son of
  THOMAS MACY and Sarah Hopcot.

BETHIAH PRATT was daughter of
  Joseph Pratt and Dorcas *Folger*.

Dorcas Folger was daughter of
PETER FOLGER and Mary Morrell.

JUDITH COFFIN was daughter of
Richard Coffin and Ruth *Bunker*.
Richard Coffin was son of
John Coffin, Esq., and Hope *Gardner*.
John Coffin, Esq., was son of
JAMES COFFIN and Mary Severance.
James Coffin was son of
TRISTRAM COFFIN and Dionis Stevens.

DEBORAH COFFIN was daughter of
LIEUTENANT JOHN COFFIN and Deborah *Austin*.
Lieutenant John Coffin was son of
TRISTRAM COFFIN and Dionis Stevens.

DEBORAH GARDNER was daughter of
RICHARD GARDNER and Sarah *Shattuck*.
Richard Gardner was son of
GOVERNOR THOMAS GARDINER.

RUTH BUNKER was daughter of
Jonathan Bunker and Elizabeth *Coffin*.
Jonathan Bunker was son of
William Bunker and Mary *Macy*.
Mary Macy was daughter of
THOMAS MACY and Sarah Hopcot.

HOPE GARDNER was daughter of
RICHARD GARDNER and Sarah *Shattuck*.
Richard Gardner was son of
THOMAS GARDINER.

DEBORAH AUSTIN was daughter of
   Joseph Austin and Sarah *Starbuck*.
Sarah Starbuck was daughter of
   EDWARD STARBUCK and Katharine Reynolds.

ELIZABETH COFFIN was daughter of
   JAMES COFFIN and Mary Severance.

Descendants from Peleg Mitchell, Sr., and Lydia
Cartwright descend also from:
Thomas Macy, twice.
Peter Folger.
James Coffin, twice.
Lieutenant John Coffin.
Tristram Coffin, four times.
Edward Starbuck, three times.
Richard Gardner, twice.
Thomas Gardiner, twice.

Mrs. Mary A. Woodbridge, daughter of Judge Brayton and Love (Mitchell) Brayton, and grand-daughter
of Peleg Mitchell, Sr., and Lydia (Cartwright) Mitchell, was a lineal descendant (on the maternal side) of
all of the above-named settlers of Nantucket,
and on the paternal of
   Christopher Hussey.
She was the first president of the Woman's Christian
Temperance Union of Ohio, and later recording secretary of the National and World's Temperance Unions,
and gave her time and her life (dying while in the service of the Union) to the cause which she had espoused.
   While she was an enthusiast, she was in no sense
fanatic, being governed always by strong common
sense, and a dignity which was nature's gift.

She travelled extensively, and often addressed large audiences, in addition to her close and conscientious work with the pen in the discharge of her duties as secretary.

Professor Maria Mitchell (see chapter on Peter Folger) was another grand-daughter of Peleg Mitchell, Sr., and Lydia (Cartwright) Mitchell.

RUSSELL FAMILY.

John Russell, Jr., married Hepzibah *Coleman*.

JOHN RUSSELL, JR., was son of
   John Russell, Sr., and Ruth *Starbuck*.
John Russell, Sr., was son of
   Daniel Russell and Deborah *Macy*.

RUTH STARBUCK was daughter of
   Nathaniel Starbuck, Jr., and Dinah *Coffin*.
Nathaniel Starbuck, Jr. was son of
   Nathaniel Starbuck, Sr., and Mary *Coffin*.
Nathaniel Starbuck, Sr., was son of
   EDWARD STARBUCK and Katharine Reynolds.

DEBORAH MACY was daughter of
   John Macy and Deborah *Gardner*.
John Macy was son of
   THOMAS MACY and Sarah Hopcot.

DINAH COFFIN was daughter of
JAMES COFFIN and Mary Severance.

MARY COFFIN was daughter of
TRISTRAM COFFIN and Dionis Stevens.

DEBORAH GARDNER was daughter of
RICHARD GARDNER and Sarah *Shattuck*.
Richard Gardner was son of
THOMAS GARDINER.

HEPZIBAH COLEMAN was daughter of
Barnabas Coleman and Rachel *Hussey*.
Barnabas Coleman was son of
John Coleman, Jr., and Priscilla *Starbuck*.
John Coleman, Jr., was son of
John Coleman, Sr., and Joanna *Folger*.
John Coleman, Sr., was son of
THOMAS COLEMAN.

RACHEL HUSSEY was daughter of
Sylvanus Hussey and Abial *Brown*.
Sylvanus Hussey was son of
STEPHEN HUSSEY and Martha Bunker.
Stephen Hussey was son of
CHRISTOPHER HUSSEY and Theodate *Batchelder*.

PRISCILLA STARBUCK was daughter of
Nathaniel Starbuck and Mary *Coffin*.
Nathaniel Starbuck was son of
EDWARD STARBUCK and Katharine Reynolds.

JOANNA FOLGER was daughter of
PETER FOLGER and Mary Morrell.

ABIAL BROWN was daughter of
John Brown and Rachel *Gardner*.
John Brown was son of
John Brown and Hannah *Hobart*.

THEODATE BATCHELDER was daughter of
REV. STEPHEN BATCHELDER.

MARY COFFIN was daughter of
TRISTRAM COFFIN and Dionis Stevens.

RACHEL GARDNER was daughter of
CAPTAIN JOHN GARDNER and Priscilla Grafton.
John Gardner was son of
THOMAS GARDINER.

HANNAH HOBART was daughter of
REV. PETER HOBART, who was son of
EDMUND HOBART.

Descendants of John Russell and Hepzibah (Coleman) Russell descend also from:
Edward Starbuck, twice.
Thomas Macy.
James Coffin.
Tristram Coffin, three times.
Richard Gardner.
John Gardner.
Thomas Gardiner, twice.
Thomas Coleman.
Christopher Hussey.
Peter Folger.
Rev. Stephen Batchelder.
Rev. Peter Hobart.
Edmund Hobart.

BARKER FAMILY.

Robert Barker married 1st, Jedidah Chase; 2d, Sarah Gardner, widow of Hezikiah Gardner, and daughter of Abishai Folger and Sarah (Mayhew).

Children of the first wife were:
Judith Barker.
Margaret Barker.
Lydia Barker.
Mary Barker.
Robert Barker.
James Barker.
Francis Barker.

Children of the second wife were:
Jedidah Barker.
Mary Barker.
Abraham Barker.
Sarah Barker.
Isaac Barker.
Jacob Barker.

ROBERT BARKER was son of
Samuel Barker and Bethiah *Folger.*
Samuel Barker was son of
Isaac Barker and Judith *Prence.*

BETHIAH FOLGER was daughter of
John Folger and Mary[2] *Barnard.*
John Folger was son of
PETER FOLGER and Mary (Morrell).

JUDITH PRENCE was daughter of
  THOMAS PRENCE and Mary *Collier.*
Mary Collier was daughter of
  WILLIAM COLLIER.

MARY[2] BARNARD was daughter of
  Nathaniel Barnard and Mary[1] *Barnard.*
Nathaniel Barnard was son of
  THOMAS BARNARD and Eleanor Barnard.

MARY[1] BARNARD was daughter of
  ROBERT BARNARD and Joanna Harvey.

JEDIDAH CHASE, first wife of Robert Barker, was
    daughter of
  James Chase and Rachel *Brown.*
James Chase was son of
  LIEUTENANT ISAAC CHASE and Mary Perkins.

RACHEL BROWN was daughter of
  John Brown and Rachel *Gardner.*
John Brown was son of
  Elder John Brown and Hannah *Hobart.*

RACHEL GARDNER was daughter of
  CAPTAIN JOHN GARDNER and Priscilla Grafton.
John Gardner was son of
  THOMAS GARDINER.

Hannah Hobart was daughter of
  REV. PETER HOBART, who was son of
  EDMUND HOBART.

Descendants from Robert Barker and Jedidah Chase
descend also from :
Peter Folger.
Thomas Prence.
William Collier.
Thomas Barnard.
Robert Barnard.
John Gardner.
Rev. Peter Hobart.
Edmund Hobart.
Thomas Gardiner.
Lieutenant Isaac Chase.

Sarah Gardner, widow of Hezikiah Gardner and
second wife of Robert Barker, was daughter of
Abishai Folger and Sarah Mayhew.*

Descendants from Robert Barker and Sarah (Gard-
ner) descend also from :
Peter Folger, twice.
Thomas Prence.
William Collier.
Thomas Barnard.
Robert Barnard.
Thomas Mayhew, Sr.
Thomas Mayhew, Jr.
Thomas Gardiner, twice.
Richard Gardner, twice.
James Coffin.
Tristram Coffin.
Thomas Macy.

---

* For details see " Family of Lucretia Mott," p. 94.
Note.—Members of the Barker family have intermarried with the
families of Hazard, of Rhode Island; Hopkins, of Baltimore;

SWAIN FAMILY.

Francis Swain, Jr., married Lydia Barker.

FRANCIS SWAIN, JR., was son of
Francis Swain, Sr., and Mary *Paddack*.
Francis Swain, Sr., was son of
John Swain, 3d, and Mary Swett.
John Swain, 3d, was son of
John Swain, 2d, and Experience *Folger*.
John Swain, 2d, was son of
JOHN SWAYNE, or Swain, 1st, and Mary Wier.
John Swain, 1st, was son of
RICHARD SWAIN and Elizabeth ——.

MARY PADDACK was daughter of
Nathaniel Paddack and Ann *Bunker*.
Ann Bunker was daughter of
William Bunker and Mary *Macy*.
Mary Macy was daughter of
THOMAS MACY and Sarah Hopcot.

EXPERIENCE FOLGER was daughter of
PETER FOLGER.

Descendants from Francis Swain and Lydia Barker,
descend also on the paternal side from :
Peter Folger.
Thomas Macy.
John Swayne.

Wharton, of Philadelphia; Sigourney, of Boston; and Baron Schön-
berg, of Germany; also with the families of Butler, of New York;
Mellor and Kirkbride, of Pennsylvania; Swain, Farnum, Newhall,
Allen, Alden, Rotch, Farrar, and Ward, of New England.

On the Maternal side from:
Lieutenant Isaac Chase.
Peter Folger.
Thomas Prence.
William Collier.
Thomas Barnard.
Robert Barnard.
John Gardner.
Thomas Gardiner.
Peter Hobart.
Edmund Hobart.

FAMILY OF LUCRETIA MOTT.

Thomas Coffin married Anna Folger.

THOMAS COFFIN was son of
  Benjamin Coffin and Deborah *Macy*.
Benjamin Coffin was son of
  Nathaniel Coffin and Damaris *Gayer*.
Nathaniel Coffin was son of
  JAMES COFFIN and Mary Severance.
James Coffin was son of
  TRISTRAM COFFIN and Dionis Stevens.

DEBORAH MACY was daughter of
  Thomas Macy and Deborah *Coffin*.
Thomas Macy was son of
  John Macy and Deborah *Gardner*.
John Macy was son of
  THOMAS MACY and Sarah Hopcot.

DAMARIS GAYER was daughter of
William Gayer and Dorcas *Starbuck.*
Dorcas Starbuck was daughter of
EDWARD STARBUCK and Katharine Reynolds.

DEBORAH COFFIN was daughter of
LIEUTENANT JOHN COFFIN and Deborah *Austin.*
Lieutenant John Coffin was son of
TRISTRAM COFFIN and Dionis Stevens.

DEBORAH GARDNER was daughter of
RICHARD GARDNER and Sarah *Shattuck.*
Richard Gardner was son of
THOMAS GARDINER.

DEBORAH AUSTIN was daughter of
Joseph Austin and Sarah *Starbuck.*
Sarah Starbuck was daughter of
EDWARD STARBUCK and Katharine Reynolds.

ANNA FOLGER was daughter of
William Folger and Ruth *Coffin.*
William Folger was son of
Abishai Folger and Sarah *Mayhew.*
Abishai Folger was son of
Nathan Folger and Sarah Church.
Nathan Folger was son of
Eleazer Folger and Sarah *Gardner.*
Eleazer Folger was son of
PETER FOLGER and Mary Morrell.

RUTH COFFIN was daughter of
Richard Coffin and Ruth *Bunker.*
Richard Coffin was son of
John Coffin, Esq., and Hope *Gardner.*

John Coffin, Esq., was son of
  JAMES COFFIN and Mary Severance.
James Coffin was son of
  TRISTRAM COFFIN and Dionis Stevens.

SARAH MAYHEW was daughter of
  Paine Mayhew and Mary Rankin.
Paine Mayhew was son of
  Matthew Mayhew.
Matthew Mayhew was son of
  THOMAS MAYHEW, JR., and Jane Paine.
Thomas Mayhew, Jr., was son of
  THOMAS MAYHEW, SR.

SARAH GARDNER was daughter of
  RICHARD GARDNER and Sarah *Shattuck.*
Richard Gardner was son of
  THOMAS GARDINER.

RUTH BUNKER was daughter of
  Jonathan Bunker and Elizabeth *Coffin.*
Jonathan Bunker was son of
  William Bunker and Mary *Macy.*
Mary Macy was daughter of
  THOMAS MACY and Sarah Hopcot.

HOPE GARDNER was daughter of
  RICHARD GARDNER and Sarah *Shattuck.*
Richard Gardner was son of
  THOMAS GARDINER.

ELIZABETH COFFIN was daughter of
  JAMES COFFIN and Mary Severance.

James Coffin was son of
TRISTRAM COFFIN and Dionis Stevens.

Descendants from Thomas Coffin and Anna Folger descend also from :
Tristram Coffin, four times.
James Coffin, three times.
John Coffin, Esq.
Peter Folger.
Richard Gardner, three times.
Thomas Gardiner, three times.
Thomas Mayhew, Sr.
Thomas Mayhew, Jr.
Edward Starbuck, twice.
Thomas Macy, twice.
Lieutenant John Coffin.

The children of Thomas and Anna (Folger) Coffin were :
Sally Coffin, unmarried.
Lucretia Coffin, married James Mott.
Eliza Coffin, married Benjamin H. Yarnall,* of Philadelphia.

---

* Descendants of Thomas Gardiner may be found in another branch of the Yarnall family.
    Edward Yarnall married Caroline R. Cope.
Caroline R. Cope was daughter of
    Thomas Pim Cope and Mary Drinker.
Mary Drinker was daughter of
    John Drinker and Rachel Reynear.
John Drinker was son of
    Henry Drinker and Mary Gottier.
Henry Drinker was son of
    Joseph Drinker and Mary Janney.
Joseph Drinker was son of
    John Drinker, of Beverly, Massachusetts, and Ruth Balch.

Mary Coffin, married Solomon Temple.

Martha Coffin, married Peter Pelham, of Kentucky, a captain in the United States army.

Thomas M. Coffin, unmarried (the only son).

FAMILIES OF THOMAS EARLE AND JOHN MILTON EARLE.

Uriel Hussey married Phebe Folger.

Tristram Hussey married Sarah Folger.

Uriel Hussey was son of George Hussey.

Tristram Hussey was son of Batchelder or Bachiler Hussey.

GEORGE HUSSEY * and BATCHELDER HUSSEY were brothers, and sons of

Sylvanus Hussey, Sr., and Hepzibah *Starbuck*.

Sylvanus Hussey was son of

STEPHEN HUSSEY and Martha Bunker.

Ruth Balch was daughter of

Benjamin Balch, the first child born in the Massachusetts Bay Colony.

Benjamin Balch married Sarah Gardiner, daughter of THOMAS GARDINER. Benjamin Balch, of Salem, was son of John and Anice Balch, a Somersetshire family which dated from the Conquest. Benjamin Balch was living in 1706.

* George Hussey's wife was Deborah Paddack, a descendant of Zechariah Paddack, who married Deborah Sears, of Yarmouth, a daughter of Richard Sears. Richard Sears married Dorothy Thatcher.

Stephen Hussey was son of
CHRISTOPHER HUSSEY and Theodate *Batchelder*.

HEPZIBAH STARBUCK was daughter of
Nathaniel Starbuck, Jr., and Dinah *Coffin*.
Nathaniel Starbuck, Jr., was son of
Nathaniel Starbuck, Sr., and Mary *Coffin*.
Nathaniel Starbuck, Sr., was son of
EDWARD STARBUCK and Katharine Reynolds.

DINAH COFFIN was daughter of
JAMES COFFIN and Mary Severance.
James Coffin was son of
TRISTRAM COFFIN and Dionis Stevens.

MARY COFFIN was daughter of
TRISTRAM COFFIN and Dionis Stevens.

THEODATE BATCHELDER was daughter of
REV. STEPHEN BATCHELDER.

Phebe Folger, } sisters, were sisters also of Anna
Sarah Folger, }
Folger (the mother of Lucretia Mott), and their de-
scent from early settlers of Nantucket, being identical
with that of Anna Folger, will be found on a previous
page, under "Family of Lucretia Mott."
Uriel Hussey's daughter Mary married Thomas
Earle; Tristram Hussey's daughter Sarah married
John Milton Earle.
Descendants from them descend also from:
Edward Starbuck.
Christopher Hussey.
Stephen Hussey.

Rev. Stephen Batchelder.
Peter Folger.
James Coffin, twice.
Tristram Coffin, twice.
Thomas Mayhew, Sr.
Thomas Mayhew, Jr.
Richard Gardner, twice.
Thomas Gardiner, twice.
Thomas Macy.

Children of Thomas and Mary Earle have intermarried with the families of Van Leer, of Chester
County; Earle, of Massachusetts; Gibbons, of Pennsylvania; and White, of Londonderry, Ireland.

SWIFT FAMILY.

Dr. Paul Swift married Dorcas Gardner.

DORCAS GARDNER was daughter of
  Zenas Gardner and Susanna *Hussey*.
Zenas Gardner was son of
  Paul Gardner and Rachel *Starbuck*.
Paul Gardner was son of
  Solomon Gardner and Anna *Coffin*.
Solomon Gardner was son of
  Richard Gardner, 2d, and Mary *Austin*.
Richard Gardner, 2d, was son of
  RICHARD GARDNER and Sarah *Shattuck*.
Richard Gardner was son of
  THOMAS GARDINER.

SUSANNA HUSSEY was daughter of
George Hussey and Deborah *Paddack*.
George Hussey was son of
Sylvanus Hussey, Sr., and Hepzibah *Starbuck*.
Sylvanus Hussey, Sr., was son of
STEPHEN HUSSEY and Martha Bunker.
Stephen Hussey was son of
CHRISTOPHER HUSSEY and Theodate *Batchelder*.*

RACHEL STARBUCK was daughter of
Thomas Starbuck and Rachel *Allen*.
Thomas Starbuck was son of
Jethro Starbuck and Dorcas *Gayer*.
Jethro Starbuck was son of
Nathaniel Starbuck and Mary *Coffin*.
Nathaniel Starbuck was son of
EDWARD STARBUCK and Katharine Reynolds.

ANNA COFFIN was daughter of
Stephen Coffin and Mary Bunker.
Stephen Coffin was son of
TRISTRAM COFFIN and Dionis Stevens.

MARY AUSTIN was daughter of
Joseph Austin and Sarah *Starbuck*.
Sarah Starbuck was daughter of
EDWARD STARBUCK and Katharine Reynolds.

DEBORAH PADDACK was daughter of
Daniel Paddack and Susanna *Gorham*.
Susanna Gorham was daughter of
Stephen Gorham and Elizabeth *Gardner*.

---

* Various spellings found in old records.

Elizabeth Gardner was daughter of
   James Gardner and Mary *Starbuck.*
James Gardner was son of
   RICHARD GARDNER and Sarah *Shattuck.*
Richard Gardner was son of
   Governor Thomas Gardiner.

HEPZIBAH STARBUCK was daughter of
   Nathaniel Starbuck, Jr., and Dinah *Coffin.*
Nathaniel Starbuck, Jr., was son of
   Nathaniel Starbuck, Sr., and Mary *Coffin.*
Nathaniel Starbuck, Sr., was son of
   EDWARD STARBUCK and Katharine Reynolds.

THEODATE BATCHELDER was daughter of
   REV. STEPHEN BATCHELDER.

RACHEL ALLEN was daughter of
   Edward Allen and Ann *Coleman.*
Ann Coleman was daughter of
   Joseph Coleman and Ann Bunker.
Joseph Coleman was son of
   THOMAS COLEMAN and Susanna ——.

DORCAS GAYER was daughter of
   William Gayer and Dorcas *Starbuck.*
Dorcas Starbuck was daughter of
   EDWARD STARBUCK and Katharine Reynolds.

MARY COFFIN was daughter of
   TRISTRAM COFFIN and Dionis Stevens (occurs
   three times).

Mary Starbuck was daughter of
  Nathaniel Starbuck, Sr., and Mary *Coffin*.
Nathaniel Starbuck, Sr., was son of
  EDWARD STARBUCK and Katharine Reynolds.

DINAH COFFIN was daughter of
  JAMES COFFIN and Mary Severance.
James Coffin was son of
  TRISTRAM COFFIN and Dionis Stevens.

Daniel Paddack was son of
  Nathaniel Paddack and Ann *Bunker*.
Ann Bunker was daughter of
  William Bunker and Mary *Macy* and grand-
  daughter of THOMAS MACY.

Descendants of Dr. Paul Swift and Dorcas Gardner
descend also from :
  Richard Gardner, twice.
  Governor Thomas Gardiner, twice.
  Stephen Hussey.
  Christopher Hussey.
  Edward Starbuck, five times.
  Tristram Coffin, four times.
  Rev. Stephen Batchelder.
  Thomas Coleman.
  Thomas Macy.
  James Coffin.

Paul Swift was born in Sandwich, Massachusetts,
1794. He was for some time a physician at Nantucket,
where he is still remembered and respected.
  In 1841 he moved to Philadelphia, where he practised medicine until 1853, when he was appointed a

teacher at Haverford School (soon after made a college); he remained there until 1865, when he resigned on account of ill health. He died in Philadelphia in 1866.

Daughters of Dr. Paul Swift and Dorcas (Gardner) Swift were:

Mary, married, 1846, Mr. Edwin Lamson, of Boston.

Katharine, married 1st, Dr. Marcus A. Moore, of Boston; 2d, Robert Wharton.

Susan, married Mr. Albert H. Franciscus, of Philadelphia.

Elizabeth, married Mr. John E. Phillips, of Baltimore.*

ROTCH FAMILY.

William Rotch married Elizabeth Barney, of Nantucket.

William Rotch was born on Nantucket, 1734, and died in New Bedford, 1828.

He was son of
    Joseph Rotch and Love *Macy.*
Joseph Rotch was son of
    William Rotch.

---

* John Howland and John Tilley, "Mayflower" passengers, are among the ancestors of this family; John Howland was a soldier in the Plymouth Military Company in 1643, and filled many other important offices.

Love Macy was daughter of
  Thomas³ Macy and Deborah *Coffin*.
Thomas Macy was son of
  John Macy and Deborah *Gardner*.
John Macy was son of
  Thomas Macy and Sarah Hopcot.

Deborah Coffin was daughter of
  Lieutenant John Coffin and Deborah *Austin*.
Lieutenant John Coffin was son of
  Tristram Coffin and Dionis Stevens.

Deborah Gardner was daughter of
  Richard Gardner and Sarah *Shattuck*.
Richard Gardner was son of
  Thomas Gardiner.

Deborah Austin was daughter of
  Joseph Austin and Sarah *Starbuck*.
Sarah Starbuck was daughter of
  Edward Starbuck.

Elizabeth Barney was daughter of
  Benjamin Barney and Lydia *Starbuck*.
Lydia Starbuck was daughter of
  Jethro Starbuck and Dorcas *Gayer*.
Jethro Starbuck was son of
  Nathaniel Starbuck and Mary Coffin.
Nathaniel Starbuck was son of
  Edward Starbuck and Katharine Reynolds.

Mary Coffin was daughter of
  Tristram Coffin and Dionis Stevens.

DORCAS GAYER was daughter of
  William Gayer and Dorcas *Starbuck.*
Dorcas Starbuck was daughter of
  EDWARD STARBUCK and Katharine Reynolds.

Descendants from William and Elizabeth (Barney)
Rotch * descend also from :

---

* Elizabeth Rotch, daughter of William and Elizabeth (Barney)
Rotch, married Samuel Rodman, of Newport.

Samuel Rodman's Sister Anna married Thomas Hazzard. Elizabeth Hazzard (b. 1783), daughter of Thomas and Anna (Rodman)
Hazzard, married Jacob Barker, son of Robert Barker.

Mrs. Eliza Farrar, wife of Professor Farrar, was a daughter of
Benjamin Rotch, of Nantucket. Benjamin Rotch married a Barker,
also of Nantucket.

Joseph Rotch was born in Salisbury, England, May 6, 1704, and
went to Nantucket, subsequently to New Bedford, where he died,
November 24, 1784.

He inaugurated the business of whale fishery so successfully
carried on by his son.

When the Revolutionary War broke out the whaling business was
practically ruined, and William Rotch went to England, hoping to
pursue the business there, but, meeting with little encouragement,
he finally went to Dunkirk, France, where special privileges from
the French government were granted him.

He carried on the business there until 1794, when he returned to
Nantucket, and after a year's residence on the island, went to New
Bedford and resided there until his death in 1828. His great-grand-
son, now living in New Bedford, says, " He was a consistent Friend
and had the courage of his convictions. I have heard my great-
aunt Mary Rotch tell the following story :

" He was at Dunkirk at the time of the Napoleonic Wars ; one
day there came news of the great victory of Austerlitz.

" Municipal orders were issued commanding every one to illumi-
nate in honor of the event.——My great grandfather was true to his
principles and refused to obey the order, though every house in the
street was a blaze of light.

" The good mayor of the city was very friendly with my grandfather and called to expostulate and if possible pursuade him—fear-

Thomas Macy.
Lieutenant John Coffin.
Tristram Coffin, twice.
Richard Gardner.
Thomas Gardiner.
Edward Starbuck, three times.

BUNKER FAMILY.

Nathan² Bunker married Elizabeth Thorne Clement.

NATHAN² BUNKER was son of
Nathan Bunker and Hepsibeth Pinkham.
Nathan¹ Bunker was son of
Shubael Bunker and Lydia *Paddack*.
Shubael Bunker was son of
Zacariah Bunker and Desire *Gorham*.

---

ing danger from the mob in those excited times, but Mr. Rotch refused.

"Well, said the Mayor finally, the street belongs to the city, and I will do what I can, so he sent and procured two large lanterns, and had them placed directly in front of the house, and detailed some Gendarmes to walk up and down in front and explain to the people that those who lived there were not enemies, but good friendly people, who did not believe in war.

"His daughter Elizabeth Rotch was a remarkable woman, living to the advanced age of ninety-nine, and when over ninety had never used the back of a chair, but sat erect without support."

William Rotch is thus described by this grandson, who saw him when he himself was only four years of age: "He was a tall venerable man with white hair and beard, and came into the room leaning on the back of a large arm chair on castors, attended by his black servant."

Zacariah Bunker was son of
  Jonathan Bunker and Elizabeth *Coffin*.
Jonathan Bunker was son of
  William Bunker and Mary *Macy*.

LYDIA PADDACK was daughter of
  Daniel Paddack and Susanna *Gorham*.
Daniel Paddack was son of
  Nathaniel Paddack and Ann *Bunker*.

DESIRE GORHAM was daughter of
  Shubael Gorham and Puella *Hussey*.
Puella Hussey was daughter of
  STEPHEN HUSSEY and Martha Bunker.
Stephen Hussey was son of
  CHRISTOPHER HUSSEY and Theodate *Batchelder*.

ELIZABETH COFFIN was daughter of
  JAMES COFFIN and Mary Severance.
JAMES COFFIN was son of
  TRISTRAM COFFIN and Dionis Stevens.

MARY MACY was daughter of
  THOMAS MACY and Sarah Hopcot.

SUSANNA GORHAM was daughter of
  Stephen Gorham and Elizabeth *Gardner*.
Elizabeth Gardner was daughter of
  James Gardner and Mary *Starbuck*.
James Gardner was son of
  RICHARD GARDNER and Sarah *Shattuck*.
Richard Gardner was son of
  THOMAS GARDINER.

ANN BUNKER was daughter of
William Bunker and Mary *Macy*.

MARY STARBUCK was daughter of
Nathaniel Starbuck and Mary *Coffin*.
Nathaniel Starbuck was son of
EDWARD STARBUCK and Katharine Reynolds.

MARY COFFIN was daughter of
TRISTRAM COFFIN and Dionis Stevens.

THEODATE BATCHELDER was daughter of
REV. STEPHEN BATCHELDER.

Descendants from Nathan Bunker and Elizabeth
Thorne Clement descend also from :
Tristram Coffin, Sr., twice.
James Coffin.
Thomas Macy, twice.
Richard Gardner.
Thomas Gardiner.
Stephen Hussey.
Christopher Hussey.
Edward Starbuck.
Rev. Stephen Batchelder.

Note.—Descendants of Nathan Bunker descend from George and
Jane Godfrey Bunker three times ; this family was of Huguenot origin. The name formerly was Bon Cœur. Upon the ancestral records
of this family we find also John Tilley and John Howland, signers of
the Mayflower Compact, adding another link between Plymouth
and Nantucket in colonial times.

Nathan Bunker married after the manner of Friends ; he was of
the prominent shipping firm of Lea & Bunker, who owned a large
amount of shipping in Philadelphia at the beginning of this century.
His daughter, Mary Clement Bunker, was mother of Captain Charles
Bunker Dahlgren, of the United States navy.

WING AND HATHAWAY CONNECTION WITH NANTUCKET.

Sylvanus Hussey, Jr., married 1st, Alice Gray; 2d, Lydia Wing.*

SYLVANUS HUSSEY, JR., was son of
Sylvanus Hussey, Sr., and Hepzibah *Starbuck*.
Sylvanus Hussey, Sr., was son of
STEPHEN HUSSEY and Martha Bunker.
Stephen Hussey was son of
CHRISTOPHER HUSSEY and Theodate *Batchelder*.

HEPZIBAH STARBUCK was daughter of
Nathaniel Starbuck, Jr., and Dinah *Coffin*.
Nathaniel Starbuck, Jr., was son of
Nathaniel Starbuck, Sr., and Mary *Coffin*.
Nathaniel Starbuck, Sr., was son of
EDWARD STARBUCK and Katharine Reynolds.

DINAH COFFIN was daughter of
JAMES COFFIN and Mary Severance.
James Coffin was son of
TRISTRAM COFFIN and Dionis Stevens.

MARY COFFIN was daughter of
TRISTRAM COFFIN and Dionis Stevens.

---

* Lydia Wing descended from John Wing, whose name appears in 1637 among associates to form the town of Sandwich, Massachusetts.
John Wing and his wife, Deborah Batchelder (daughter of Rev. Stephen Batchelder), sailed on the "William and Francis" from London, March 9, 1682, and arrived in Boston June 5, 1682.

LYDIA WING was daughter of
Samuel Wing and Hepzibah Hathaway.
Hepzibah Hathaway was daughter of
Thomas Hathaway and Hepzibah *Starbuck*.
HEPZIBAH STARBUCK was daughter of
Nathaniel Starbuck and Mary *Coffin*.
Nathaniel Starbuck was son of
EDWARD STARBUCK and Katharine Reynolds.

MARY COFFIN was daughter of
Tristram Coffin and Dionis Stevens.

Descendants of Sylvanus Hussey and Lydia Wing
(his second wife) descend also on the paternal side
from:
Christopher Hussey.
Stephen Hussey.
Rev. Stephen Batchelder.
Edward Starbuck.
Tristram Coffin.
James Coffin.
On the maternal side from:
Edward Starbuck.
Tristram Coffin.

ABIGAIL, another daughter of Samuel and Hepzibah
(Hathaway) Wing, married Paul Wing, son of Zaccheus and Content (Swift) Wing. Hepzibah, daughter
of Paul and Abigail Wing, married Estes Newhall,
whose son Paul Wing Newhall married Hannah Johnson; members of this family descend from Edward

Starbuck and Tristram Coffin. Paul Wing and Hannah (Johnson) Newhall settled in Philadelphia.*

COGGESHALL CONNECTION WITH NANTUCKET.

Job Coggeshall married Deborah Starbuck.

DEBORAH STARBUCK was daughter of
  Tristram Starbuck and Deborah *Coffin*.
Tristram Starbuck was son of
  Nathaniel Starbuck, Jr., and Dinah *Coffin*.
Nathaniel Starbuck, Jr., was son of
  Nathaniel Starbuck, Sr., and Mary *Coffin*.
Nathaniel Starbuck, Sr., was son of
  EDWARD STARBUCK and Katharine Reynolds.

DEBORAH COFFIN was daughter of
  Samuel Coffin and Miriam *Gardner*.
Samuel Coffin was son of
  LIEUTENANT JOHN COFFIN and Deborah *Austin*.
John Coffin was son of
  TRISTRAM COFFIN and Dionis Stevens.

---

* A great-grand-daughter of Thomas and Hepzibah Hathaway married Henry A. Wisner, grandson of Henry Wisner, of Orange County, New York. The last named was a member of the Continental Congress in 1776, voted for the Declaration of Independence, and was subsequently a member of the State Committee of Safety of New York, and of the convention which formed the Constitution of New York in 1777.

DINAH COFFIN was daughter of
JAMES COFFIN and Mary Severance.
James Coffin was son of
TRISTRAM COFFIN and Dionis Stevens.

MARY COFFIN was daughter of
TRISTRAM COFFIN and Dionis Stevens.

MIRIAM GARDNER was daughter of
Richard Gardner and Mary *Austin*.*
Richard Gardner was son of
RICHARD GARDNER and Sarah *Shattuck*.
Richard Gardner was son of
THOMAS GARDINER.

DEBORAH AUSTIN was daughter of
Joseph Austin and Sarah *Starbuck*.
Sarah Starbuck was daughter of
EDWARD STARBUCK and Katharine Reynolds.

Descendants of Job Coggeshall and Deborah Star-
buck descend also from:
Edward Starbuck, three times.
Tristram Coffin, three times.
Lieutenant John Coffin.
James Coffin.
Richard Gardner.
Thomas Gardiner.

---

* Mary Austin was a sister of Deborah Austin.
Note.—Deborah Coggeshall, daughter of Job and Deborah (Starbuck) Coggeshall, married, as second wife, Paul Macy, a descendant of Thomas Macy. Other members of this family have intermarried with the families of Walter and Janney.

BUFFUM CONNECTION WITH NANTUCKET.

David Buffum, 1st, married Hepzibah Mitchell, both of Newport.

HEPZIBAH MITCHELL was daughter of
James Mitchell and Ann *Folger*.

ANN FOLGER was daughter of
Jethro Folger and Mary *Starbuck*.
Jethro Folger was son of
John Folger and Mary *Barnard*.
John Folger was son of
PETER FOLGER.

MARY STARBUCK was daughter of
Nathaniel Starbuck, Jr., and Dinah *Coffin*.
Nathaniel Starbuck, Jr., was son of
Nathaniel Starbuck, Sr., and Mary *Coffin*.
Nathaniel Starbuck, Sr., was son of
EDWARD STARBUCK and Katharine Reynolds.

MARY[2] BARNARD was daughter of
Nathaniel Barnard and Mary[1] *Barnard*.
Nathaniel Barnard was son of
THOMAS BARNARD and Eleanor ——.

DINAH COFFIN was daughter of
JAMES COFFIN and Mary Severance.
James Coffin was son of
TRISTRAM COFFIN and Dionis Stevens.

MARY COFFIN was daughter of
TRISTRAM COFFIN and Dionis Stevens.

MARY[1] BARNARD was daughter of
ROBERT BARNARD and Joanna Harvey.

Descendants of David Buffum * and Hepzibah Mitch-
ell † descend also from :
Tristram Coffin, twice.
James Coffin.
Thomas Barnard.
Robert Barnard.
Edward Starbuck.
Peter Folger.

---

* Members of this Buffum family married into the same Barker
family to which the Nantucket Barkers belong, having descended
from William Collier and Thomas Prence through Prince Barker,
who was son of Isaac Barker and Elizabeth Slocum, and grandson of
Isaac Barker and Judith, daughter of Governor Prence.   Elizabeth
Slocum was daughter of Peleg Slocum, who went with John Richardson to Nantucket in 1701, and with Thomas Story in 1704.   Peleg
Slocum's wife was Mary Holder, daughter of Christopher Holder,
the Quaker, who in 1659 was sentenced in Boston to banishment, on
pain of death.   See Besse's History.

† James Mitchell, father of Hepzibah Mitchell, was son of Richard
Mitchell and Elizabeth Tripp, of Portsmouth, Rhode Island, from
whom, also, descend the Nantucket Mitchells.

STANTON CONNECTION WITH NANTUCKET.

EDWIN MACY STANTON was son of
  David Stanton and Lucy Norman.
David Stanton was son of
  Benjamin Stanton and Abigail *Macy.*

ABIGAIL MACY was daughter of
  David Macy and Dinah *Gardner.*
David Macy was son of
  John Macy, Jr., and Judith Worth.
John Macy, Jr., was son of
  John Macy, Sr., and Deborah *Gardner.*
John Macy, Sr., was son of
  THOMAS MACY and Sarah Hopcot.

DINAH GARDNER was daughter of
  Solomon Gardner and Anna *Coffin.*
Solomon Gardner was son of
  Richard Gardner, Jr., and Mary *Austin.*
Richard Gardner, Jr., was son of
  RICHARD GARDNER, SR., and Sarah *Shattuck.*
Richard Gardner, Sr., was son of
  THOMAS GARDINER.

DEBORAH GARDNER was daughter of
  RICHARD GARDNER and Sarah *Shattuck.*
Richard Gardner was son of
  THOMAS GARDINER.

ANNA COFFIN was daughter of
  Stephen Coffin and Mary Bunker.
Stephen Coffin was son of
  TRISTRAM COFFIN and Dionis Stevens.

MARY AUSTIN was daughter of
  Joseph Austin and Sarah Starbuck.
Sarah Starbuck was daughter of
  EDWARD STARBUCK and Katharine Reynolds.

Therefore Edwin Macy Stanton and all descendants
from Benjamin Stanton and Abigail Macy descend also
from :
Thomas Macy.
Richard Gardner, twice.
Thomas Gardiner, twice.
Tristram Coffin.
Edward Starbuck.

Note.—Zaccheus Macy, son of Zaccheus and seventh in descent
from Thomas Macy, married Sarah, daughter of Giles E. and
Hannah (Beebe) Stanton, of New Bedford.

APPENDIX.

Adams, Alexander, *m.* Mary Coffin.* (Savage, vol. i. p. 8, 1652.)

Barnard, Nathaniel, son Thomas and Eleanor Barnard, *m.* Mary Barnard, dau. Robert and Joanna Barnard. (W. C. Folger MSS.)

Barnard, Nathaniel, Jr., *m.* Judith Folger, widow Peter Folger[2] and dau. Stephen Coffin. (Ibid.)

Barnard, Nathaniel, 3d, *m.* Hepzibah Hussey, dau. Sylvanus Hussey. (Ibid.)

Barney, Benjamin, son Jonathan and Sarah Barney, Rhode Island, *m.* 1st, Lydia Starbuck, dau. Jethro and Dorcas Starbuck (Nantucket Friends' Records, Bk. I. p. 28, 1722); 2d, Huldah Bunker, widow Simeon and dau. Bachilor Hussey (Ibid., p. 221).

Barney, Benjamin, son Benjamin and Lydia Barney, *m.* Jemima Jenkins, dau. Peter and Abigail Jenkins. (Ibid., p. 217, 1753.)

Barney, Jonathan, *m.* Abial Coffin, dau. Barnabas Coffin. (W. C. Folger MSS.)

Barney, Jacob, of Newport, *m.* Dorcas Barnard, dau. Nathaniel and Dorcas Barnard. (Nantucket Town Records, Bk. I. p. 34, 1726.)

Barney, Phebe, dau. Benjamin and Huldah (Bunker) Barney, *m.* Joseph Swain. (W. C. Folger MSS., Barney Family.)

Barker, Isaac, *m.* Judith Prence, dau. Gov. Thomas Prence. (Winsor's History of Duxbury, 1665.)

Barker, Samuel, son Isaac and Judith Barker, *m.* Bethiah Folger, dau. John and Mary (Barnard) Folger. (Savage, vol. i. p. 115, 1718.)

Barker, Isaac, son Isaac and Judith (Prence) Barker, *m.* Elizabeth Slocum, dau. Peleg Slocum and Mary Holder. (Family Records, 1707.)

Barker, Robert, son Samuel and Bethiah (Folger) Barker, *m.* 1st, Jedidah Chase, dau. James and grand-daughter Lieutenant Isaac Chase (Nantucket Town Records, Bk. I. p. 49, 1744); 2d, Sarah Gardner, widow Hezikiah Gardner, and dau. Abishai and Dinah (Starbuck) Folger (W. C. Folger MSS.).

---

* Mary (Coffin) Adams was a sister of Tristram Coffin, Sr. Benjamin Franklin Folger, genealogist, says she had four children, and from them descended the illustrious family of that name in Massachusetts.

CHILDREN OF ROBERT BARKER AND FIRST WIFE, JEDIDAH CHASE.

Barker, Judith, *m.* Shubael Gardner, son Reuben Gardner. (W. C. Folger MSS.)

Barker, Margaret, *m.* 1st, Paul Hussey, son George and Elizabeth Hussey (Ibid., p. 185, 1764); 2d, Thomas Jenkins (Ibid., 1808).

Barker, Lydia, *m.* Francis Swain. (Nantucket Friends' Records, 1767.)

Barker, Mary, *unm.* (W. C. Folger MSS.)

Barker, Robert. (Ibid.)

Barker, James, *m.* Sarah Coffin, dau. William and Lydia (Gardner) Coffin. (Ibid.)

Barker, Francis, *m.* Deborah Russell. (Nantucket Town Records, Bk. I. p. 120, 1776.)

CHILDREN OF ROBERT BARKER AND SECOND WIFE, SARAH GARDNER.

Barker, Jedidah, *m.* William Macy, son William and Mary (Barney) Macy. (Macy Genealogy, p. 121, 1807.)

Barker, Mary, *m.* 1st, Walter Allen (W. C. Folger MSS., 1813); 2d, Moses Farnum (Ibid., 1847).

Barker, Abraham, *m.* Priscilla Hopkins, of Baltimore. (Ibid.)

Barker, Sarah, *m.* Andrew Sigourney, of Boston. (Ibid.)

Barker, Isaac, *unm.* (Ibid.)

Barker, Jacob,* *m.* Elizabeth Hazzard, dau. Thomas and Anna Hazzard. (Gen. of Rodman Family, No. 331, pp. 78, 74, 1801.)

---

* CHILDREN OF JACOB BARKER AND ELIZABETH HAZZARD.

Barker, Robert, died in infancy.

Barker, Robert, *unm.*

Barker, Thomas, *unm.*

Barker, William, *m.* Jeanette James.

Barker, Andrew Sigourney, *unm.*

Barker, Anna Hazzard, *m.* Samuel Gray Ward.

Barker, Jacob, *unm.*

Barker, Elizabeth Hazzard, *m.* 1st, Baldwin Brower; 2d, William T. Van Zandt; 3d, John McCaulis.

Barker, Sarah, *m.* 1st, John C. Harrison; 2d, William H. Hunt.

Barker, Abraham, *m.* 1st, Sarah Wharton, 1842; 2d, Katharine Crane, 1871.

Barker, Mary, died young.

Barker, John W., died young.

Brown, John (Elder), *m.* Hannah Hobart, dau. Peter Hobart.*
(Savage, vol. i. p. 271, 1658.)

Brown, John, *m.* Rachel Gardner, dau. Capt. John Gardner.
(Ibid., vol. ii. p. 288.)

Brock, John, *m.* Merib Mitchell. (Nantucket Town Records,
Bk. I. p. 148, 1800.)

Buffum, David, Sr., *m.* Hepzibah Mitchell. (Family Records,
1784.)

Bunker, Elizabeth, *m.* Thomas Look, of Tisbury. (W. C. Folger,
Bunker Family, p. 60, 1646.)

Bunker, William, *m.* Mary Macy, dau. Thomas Macy and Sarah
Hopcot. (Nantucket Town Records, Bk. I. p. 1, 1669.)

Bunker, Nathan, *m.* Elizabeth Thorne Clement. (Family Record,
1813.)

Bunker, Nathan, *m.* Hepsibeth Pinkham. (Ibid., 1781.)

Bunker, Shubael, *m.* Lydia Paddack. (Ibid., 1751.)

Bunker, Zachariah, *m.* Desire Gorham (by John Coffin, justice of
peace). (Nantucket Town Records, Bk. I. p. 23, 1728.)

Bunker, Jonathan, son William Bunker, *m.* Elizabeth Coffin.
(J. Osborne Austin's "One Hundred and Sixty Allied Families,"
p. 49.)

Bunker, George, son William Bunker, *m.* Deborah Coffin. (Ibid.,
1695.)

Bunker, Ann, daughter William Bunker, *m.* Joseph Coleman.
(Ibid.)

Butler, William, *m.* Eunice Coffin.† (Savage, vol. i. p. 8.)

Butler, William, *m.* Mary Jenkins (by Josiah Coffin, justice of
peace). (Nantucket Town Records, Bk. I. p. 56, 1747.)

Cartwright, Sampson, *m.* Bethiah Pratt. (W. C. Folger MSS.)

Cartwright, Hezidiah, *m.* Abigail Brown (by John Coffin, justice
of peace). (Nantucket Town Records Bk. I. p. 28, 1781-82.)

Cartwright, James, *m.* Love Macy (second wife). (Records of
Friends, Nantucket, Massachusetts, 1759.)

Coffin, Tristram, Sr.,‡ *m.* Dionis Stevens. (N. E. Hist. and Gen.
Reg., vol. xxiv. pp. 151, 152, 1630.)

---

* See pages 58, 59, for Peter Hobart.

† Eunice Coffin was sister of Tristram Coffin, Sr.

‡ Benjamin Franklin Folger, genealogist, says, "It is worthy of
note at that period, that neither Tristram Coffin nor any of his
children married a second time."

Children of Tristram Coffin, Sr.

Coffin, Peter, *m.* Abigail Starbuck. ("One Hundred and Sixty Allied Families," p. 67, about 1656.)

Coffin, Tristram, Jr., *m.* Judith Somerby (widow Henry), dau. Edmund Greenleaf. (Ibid., 1652.)

Coffin, Elizabeth, *m.* Stephen Greenleaf. (Ibid., 1651.)

Coffin, James, *m.* Mary Severance, dau. of John Severance, of Salisbury, Massachusetts. (Ibid., p. 68, 1663.)

Coffin, Mary, *m.* Nathaniel Starbuck. (Ibid., p. 221, 1662.)

Coffin, John (Lieutenant), *m.* Deborah Austin. (N. E. Hist. and Gen. Reg., vol. xxiv. pp. 151, 152, 1668.)

Coffin, Stephen, *m.* Mary Bunker. ("Ye Coffin Family," by Allen Coffin, LL.B., p. 58, 1668–69.)

Children of Peter Coffin.

Coffin, Abigail, *m.* Daniel Davidson, of Ipswich. ("Ye Coffin Family," by Allen Coffin, LL.B., p. 53, 1673.)

Coffin, Peter, *m.* Elizabeth Starbuck, dau. Nathaniel and Mary Starbuck. (Ibid., 1682.)

Coffin, Jethro, *m.* Mary Gardner, dau. John Gardner. (Ibid.)

Coffin, Tristram, *m.* Deborah Colcord. (Ibid.)

Coffin, Robert, *m.* Joanna Dyer (widow), dau. Hon. John Gilman, of Exeter. (Ibid.)

Coffin, Edward, *m.* Anna Gardner, dau. Capt. John and Priscilla Gardner. (Ibid.)

Coffin, Elizabeth, *m.* Col. John Gilman, of Exeter. (Ibid., 1698.)

Children of Tristram Coffin, Jr.

Coffin, Judith, *m.* John Sanborn, of Hampton, New Hampshire. ("Ye Coffin Family," by Allen Coffin, LL.B., p. 54, 1674.)

Coffin, Deborah, *m.* Joseph Knight. (Ibid., 1677.)

Coffin, Mary, *m.* Joseph Little. (Ibid., 1677.)

Coffin, James, *m.* Florence Hooke. (Ibid., 1685.)

Coffin, John, *unm.* (Ibid.)

Coffin, Lydia, *m.* 1st, Moses Little (Ibid.); 2d, John Pike (Ibid., 1695).

Coffin, Enoch, *unm.* (Ibid.)

Coffin, Stephen, *m.* Sarah Atkinson. (Ibid., 1685.)

CHILDREN OF JAMES COFFIN.

Coffin, Mary, m. 1st, Richard Pinkham, of Portsmouth (came from Isle of Wight) (" Ye Coffin Family," by Allen Coffin, LL.B., p. 56) ; 2d, James Gardner, son Richard and Sarah Gardner (Ibid.).

Coffin, James, Jr., m. 1st, Love Gardner, dau. Richard and Sarah ; 2d, Ruth Gardner, dau. John and Priscilla Gardner (Ibid., 1692).

Coffin, Nathaniel, m. Damaris Gayer, dau. William and Dorcas Gayer. (Town Records of Nantucket, Bk. I. p. 5, 1692.)

Coffin, John, m. Hope Gardner, dau. Richard and Sarah Gardner. (Allen Coffin, LL.B., p. 56, 1692.)

Coffin, Dinah, m. Nathaniel Starbuck, Jr. (Savage, vol. ii. p. 229, 1690.)

Coffin, Deborah, m. George Bunker, son William and Mary Bunker. (Allen Coffin, LL.B., p. 56, 1695.)

Coffin, Ebenezer, m. Eleanor Barnard, dau. Nathaniel Barnard. (Ibid., 1700.)

Coffin, Joseph, m. Bethiah Macy, dau. John Macy. (Ibid., 1719.)

Coffin, Benjamin, unm. (Ibid.)

Coffin, Ruth, m. Joseph Gardner, son Richard[2] Gardner. (Ibid.)

Coffin, Abigail, m. Nathaniel Gardner. (Ibid.)

Coffin, Experience, unm. (Ibid.)

Coffin, Jonathan, m. Hepzibah Harker, dau. Ebenezer Harker. (Ibid.)

Coffin, Elizabeth, m. 1st, Jonathan Bunker, son William and Mary Bunker (Ibid.) ; 2d, Thomas Clark.

CHILDREN OF LIEUTENANT JOHN COFFIN.

Coffin, Lydia, m. 1st, John Logan ; 2d, John Draper; 3d, Thomas Thaxter, of Hingham. (" Ye Coffin Family," by Allen Coffin, LL.B., p. 58.)

Coffin, Peter, m. 1st, Christian Condy (Ibid.) ; 2d, Hope Macy, dau. Joseph and Bethiah (Macy) Gardner.

Coffin, Enoch, m. Beulah Eddy. (Ibid., 1700.)

Coffin, Samuel, m. Miriam Gardner, dau. Richard[2] Gardner. (Ibid., 1705.)

Coffin, Hannah, m. Benjamin Gardner, son Richard[2] Gardner. (Ibid.)

Coffin, Tristram, m. Mary Bunker, dau. William Bunker. (Ibid., 1714.)

Coffin, Deborah, m. Thomas Macy[3], son John Macy. (Ibid., 1708.)

CHILDREN OF STEPHEN COFFIN.

Coffin, Dionis, *m.* Jacob Norton. ("Ye Coffin Family," by Allen Coffin, LL.B., p. 58.)

Coffin, Peter, *m.* —— ——, in Boston. (Ibid.)

Coffin, Stephen, Jr., *m.* Experience Look, dau. Thomas Look. (Nantucket Town Records, Bk. I. p. 8, 1693.)

Coffin, Judith, *m.* 1st, Peter[3] Folger, (d. 1707) son Eleazer Folger (Allen Coffin, LL.B.); 2d, Nathaniel Barnard, son Nathaniel Barnard (Ibid., p. 58, 1718); 3d, Stephen Wilcox (W. C. Folger MSS., p. 7, 1722).

Coffin, Susanna, *m.* Peleg Bunker, son William Bunker. (Allen Coffin, LL.B., p. 58.)

Coffin, Mehitable, *m.* Armstrong Smith. (Ibid.)

Coffin, Anna, *m.* Solomon Gardner, son Richard[2] Gardner. (Ibid.)

Coffin, Hepzibah, *m.* Samuel Gardner. (Ibid.)

Coffin, Paul, *m.* Mary Allen, dau. Edward Allen. (Ibid., 1729.)

Coffin, Richard, *m.* Ruth Bunker. (N. E. Hist. and Gen. Reg., vol. xxiv. p. 306.)

Coffin, Ebenezer, *m.* Eleanor Barnard. ("One Hundred and Sixty Allied Familes," p. 68, 1700.)

Coffin, Thomas, *m.* Anna Folger. ("Life and Letters of James and Lucretia Mott," by Anna Davis Hallowell; also B. F. Folger, genealogist, 1779.)

CHILDREN OF THOMAS COFFIN AND ANNA FOLGER.

Coffin, Lucretia, *m.* James Mott, of Long Island. ("Life and Letters of James and Lucretia Mott," by Anna Davis Hallowell, 1811.)

Coffin, Eliza, *m.* Benjamin H. Yarnall, of Philadelphia. (Ibid., 1814.)

Coffin, Mary, *m.* Solomon Temple. (Ibid, 1824.)

Coffin, Martha, *m.* Peter Pelham, of Kentucky. (Ibid., 1824.)

Coffin, Thomas, *unm.*

Coffin, Nathaniel, *m.* Elizabeth Coleman. (Nantucket Friends' Records, 1757.)

Coggeshall, Joshua, *m.* 1st, Joan West (Savage vol. i. p. 422); 2d, Rebecca Russell (1677).

Coggeshall, Job, *m.*, among Friends, Deborah Starbuck. (W. C. Folger MSS., Starbuck Family, p. 61.)

Coggeshall, Caleb, *m.* Elizabeth Hosier. (Family Records, 1793.)
Coggeshall, Giles Hosier, *m.* Marianna Walters. (Ibid., 1838.)

Coleman, Thomas,* *m.* 1st, Susanna, d. 1643; 2d, Mary (widow Edmund Johnson); 3d, Margery Asbourne. (Joshua Coffin's "History of Newbury," Appendix, p. 298, 1648.)
Coleman, John, 1st, son Thomas Coleman, *m.* Joanna Folger. (William C. Folger MSS.)
Coleman, John, 2d, son John Coleman, 1st, *m.* Priscilla Starbuck. ("One Hundred and Sixty Allied Families," p. 220, 1694.)
Coleman, Dorcas,† *m.* John Tillotson. (Joshua Coffin's "History of Newbury," Appendix, p. 298.)
Coleman, Jeremiah, *m.* Sarah Pratt (by William Worth, justice of Peace). (Nantucket Town Records, Bk. I. p. 10, 1714-15.)
Coleman, Andrew, *m.* Lydia Folger. (W. C. Folger MSS., 1791.)
Coleman, Enoch, *m.* Mary Myrick. (Ibid., 1748.)
Coleman, Barnabas, son John Coleman, 2d, *m.* Rachel Hussey. (Nantucket Friends' Records, Bk. I. p. 62, 1733.)

CHILDREN OF BARNABAS COLEMAN AND RACHEL HUSSEY.

Coleman, Sarah, *m.* George Folger. (W. C. Folger MSS., 1752.)
Coleman, Abial, *m.* Timothy Folger. (Ibid., 1753.)
Coleman, Rebecca, *m.* Nathaniel Coffin. (Ibid.)
Coleman, Judith, *m.* Andrew Worth. (Ibid.)
Coleman, Seth, *m.* Deborah Swain, dau. Reuben Swain. (Nantucket Friends' Records, 1768.)
Coleman, Sylvanus, *m.* 1st, Mary Swift (Ibid., 1768); 2d, Phebe Brown (1779).
Coleman, William, *m.* 1st, Abigail Barnard (Nantucket Friends' Records, Bk. II. p. 109, 1770); 2d, Hepzibah Wing (Sandwich Friends' Records, 1780).
Coleman, Barnabas, *m.* 1st, Abial Clark, by Caleb Bunker, justice of peace (Nantucket Town Records, Bk. I. p. 106, 1776); 2d, Sarah Morse (W. C. Folger MSS.).
Coleman, Hepzibah, *m.* John Russell. (Nantucket Friends' Records, 1777).

---

* Children of Thomas Coleman were as follows: First wife, Susanna, had Benjamin, b. 1640; Joseph, b. 1642. Second wife, Mary, had Isaac, Joanna, and John. Third wife, Margery, had one son, Tobias Coleman.

† Dorcas Coleman was a sister of Thomas Coleman, the proprietor.

Coleman, Elizabeth, *m.* Abishai Folger, Jr. (W. C. Folger MSS., 1772.)

Coleman, Obed, *m.* Elizabeth Swain. (Nantucket Friends' Records, 1780.)

Cornell, William, *m.* Lydia Hussey. (Nantucket Town Records, Bk. I. p. 145, 1799.)

Earle, Thomas, *m.* Mary Hussey. (W. C. Folger, p. 184, 1820.)

Earle, John Milton, *m.* Sarah Hussey. (Ibid., 1821.)

Folger, John, *m.* Meribah Gibbs (probably second wife). (N. E. Hist. and Gen. Reg., vol. xvi., Folger Family.)

Folger, Peter, *m.* Mary Morrell. (Savage, vol. ii. pp. 177,178.)

CHILDREN OF PETER FOLGER AND MARY MORRELL.

Folger, Eleazer, *m.* Sarah Gardner, dau. Richard and Sarah (Shattuck) Gardner. (Savage, vol. ii. p. 177, 1671.)

Folger, Joanna, *m.* John Coleman. (Ibid.)

Folger, Bethiah, *m.* John Barnard, son Robert Barnard. (Ibid., 1669.)

Folger, Dorcas, *m.* Joseph Pratt. (Ibid., 1675.)

Folger, Patience, *m.* 1st, Ebenezer Harker (Savage, vol. ii. p. 177); 2d, James Gardner, as second wife (Ibid., p. 228).

Folger, Bethsua, *m.* Joseph Pope, of Salem. (Savage, vol. ii. p. 177.)

Folger, John, *m.* Mary Barnard, dau. Nathaniel Barnard. (Ibid.)

Folger, Experience, *m.* John Swain, Jr., son John Swain, the proprietor. (Ibid.)

Folger, Abiah, *m.* Josiah Franklin. (N. E. Hist. and Gen. Reg., vol. xvi., Folger Family, probably 1690.)

CHILDREN OF ELEAZER FOLGER AND SARAH GARDNER.

Folger, Eleazer, Jr., *m.* 1st, Bethia Gardner (Nantucket Town Records, Bk. I. p. 24); 2d, Mary Marshall (Ibid., p. 10, 1717).

Folger, Peter, *m.* Judith Coffin, dau. Stephen and Mary Coffin, (N. E. Hist. and Gen. Reg., vol. xvi. pp. 271–274, Folger Family.)

Folger, Nathan, *m.* Sarah Church. (Nantucket Town Records, Bk. I. p. 8, 1699.)

Folger, Sarah, *m.* Anthony Oder. (Ibid., p. 6, 1702.)

Folger, Mary, *m.* John Arthur. (Nantucket Town Records, Bk. I. p. 9, 1704.)

CHILDREN OF NATHAN FOLGER AND SARAH CHURCH.

Folger, Abishai, *m.* 1st, Sarah Mayhew W. C. Folger (MSS., 1727); 2d, Dinah Starbuck, widow Benjamin, and dau. Stephen Coffin, Jr. (Ibid.).

Folger, Peter, *m.* Christian Swain. (Nantucket Town Records, Bk. I. p. 45, 1731.)

Folger, Barzillai, *m.* Phebe Coleman. (Nantucket Friends' Records, 1730.)

Folger, Timothy, m. Anna Chase. (Nantucket Town Records, Bk. I. p. 30, 1733.)

Folger, Leah, *m.* 1st, Richard³ Gardner (Ibid., p. 16, 1724); 2d, Seth Paddack, son Joseph Paddack (W. C. Folger MSS., Gardner Family, p. 4).

Folger, Judith, *m.* Thomas Jenkins. (Nantucket Town Records, 1728–29.)

Folger, Esther, *unm.*

CHILDREN OF ABISHAI FOLGER AND SARAH MAYHEW, FIRST WIFE.

Folger, William, *m.* Ruth Coffin, dau. Barnabas Coffin. (Nantucket Friends' Records, Bk. I. p. 170, 1749.)

Folger, George, *m.* 1st, Sarah Coleman (Ibid., 1752); 2d, Sarah Shove, dau. of Barnabas.

Folger, Timothy, *m.* Abial Coleman. (Nantucket Friends' Records, 1758.)

CHILDREN OF ABISHAI FOLGER AND DINAH STARBUCK, SECOND WIFE.

Folger, Sarah, *m.* 1st, Hezekiah Gardner, (Nantucket Friends' Records, 1758); 2d, Robert Barker (W. C. Folger MSS.).

Folger, Hepzibah, *m.* Daniel Hussey, Jr. (Nantucket Friends' Records, 1760.)

Folger, Dinah, *m.* Seth Jenkins. (Geo. H. Folger MSS., p. 194.)

Folger, Abishai, *m.* Elizabeth Coleman. (Nantucket Friends' Records, 1783.)

Folger, Reuben, *m.* Phebe Folger. (Nantucket Town Records, Bk. I. p. 112, 1783.)

Folger, Robert, *m.* Elizabeth Folger, dau. Benjamin Folger. (W. C. Folger MSS., p. 9.)

CHILDREN OF WILLIAM FOLGER AND RUTH COFFIN.

Folger, Judith, m. Zaccheus Bunker, son of Zachery and Desire Bunker. (Nantucket Friends' Records, 1767.)

Folger, William, Jr., m. Susan Swain. (Nantucket Town Records, Bk. I., 1798.)

Folger, Sarah, Jr., m. Tristram Hussey. (Nantucket Friends' Records, 1777.)

Folger, Lydia, m. Zaccheus Hussey. (Nantucket Town Records, Bk. I., 1780.)

Folger, Richard, m. Sarah Pease (by George Bunker, justice of peace). (Ibid., p. 15, 1722.)

Folger, Francis, unm.

Folger, Elizabeth, m. as second wife Josiah Barker, son Josiah and Elizabeth Barker. (Nantucket Friends' Records, 1786.)

Folger, Phebe, m. Uriel Hussey. (Ibid., 1789.)

Folger, Anna, m. Thomas Coffin. (Ibid., 1790.)

Folger, Mayhew,* m. Mary Joy, dau. Francis and Phebe Joy. (Ibid., 1798.)

Folger, Walter, 1st, m. Elizabeth Starbuck, dau. Thomas and Rachel Starbuck. (W. C. Folger MSS., p. 18.)

Folger, Walter, 2d, m. Anna Ray, dau. Alexander and Elizabeth Ray. (Ibid., p. 19.)

Folger, Walter, 3d, m. Polly Folger, dau. Simeon and Phebe Folger. (Nantucket Town Records, Bk. I. p. 177, 1809.)

Folger, Dinah, m. Stephen Chase. (Ibid., p. 47, 1742.)

Folger, Judith, m. James Gardner. (Ibid., p. 52, 1746.)

Folger, Nathaniel, m. Priscilla Chase. (Ibid., 1718.)

Folger, George, Jr., son George and Sarah Folger, m. Rebecca Slocum. (W. C. Folger MSS.)

Folger, George Gill, son George, Jr., m. Anna Barker, dau. Francis Barker. (Ibid., 1807.)

Folger, Jethro, m. Mary Starbuck, dau. Nathaniel Starbuck, Jr., and Dinah (Coffin). (Nantucket Friends' Records, Bk. I. p. 6, 1710.)

Folger, Barillai, m. Miriam Gardner. (Nantucket Town Records, Bk. I. p. 163, 1808.)

Folger, Uriah, m. Anna Gardner. (Ibid., p. 157, 1803.)

---

* Captain Mayhew Folger found the lost mutineers of the ship "Bounty" on Pitcairn Island in 1809.

Folger, Lydia, *m.* Zaccheus Hussey. (Ibid., p. 109, 1780.)

Folger, Ann, *m.* James Mitchell. (See Mitchell Family Records, 1738.)

CHILDREN OF GOVERNOR THOMAS GARDINER AND MARGARET FRIER.

Gardiner, Thomas, *m.* 1st, Margaret Frier; 2d, Damaris Shattuck. ("One Hundred and Sixty Allied Families," pp. 100, 207.)

Gardner, Seeth, *m.* Joseph Grafton, 2d. (Savage, vol. ii. p. 229.)

Gardner, Richard, *m.* Sarah Shattuck. (Ibid., 1652.)

Gardner, George, *m.* Hannah Shattuck. (Ibid., p. 228.)

Gardner, John, *m.* Priscilla Grafton. (Ibid.)

Gardner, Samuel, *m.* Mary White. (Ibid., p. 230.)

Gardner, Joseph, *m.* Ann Downing, dau. Emanuel Downing. (Ibid.)

Gardner, Sarah, *m.* Benjamin Balch. (Ibid.)

Gardner, Miriam, *m.* John Hill. (Ibid.)

CHILDREN OF RICHARD GARDINER, 1ST, AND SARAH SHATTUCK.

Gardner, Joseph, *m.* Bethia Macy, dau. Thomas and Sarah (Hopcot) Macy. (Savage, vol. ii. p. 229, 1670.)

Gardner, Sarah, *m.* Eleazer Folger, son Peter and Mary (Morrell) Folger. (Ibid., 1671.)

Gardner, Richard, Jr., *m.* Mary Austin. (Ibid., p. 230, 1674, and Nantucket Town Records, Bk. I. p. 2.)

Gardner, Deborah, *m.* 1st, John Macy, son Thomas[1] Macy (Savage, vol. ii. p. 229); 2d, Stephen Pease (Macy Genealogy, p. 67).

Gardner, Damaris.

Gardner, James,* *m.* 1st, Mary Starbuck, dau. Nathaniel Starbuck, Sr.; 2d, Patience Folger, dau. Peter Folger; 3d, Rachel Brown, widow John Brown, of Salem, and dau. Capt. John Gardner; 4th, Mary Pinkham, widow Richard Pinkham, and dau. James Coffin and Mary Severance. (Savage, vol. ii. p. 227.)

Gardner, Miriam, *m.* John Worth. (Ibid., p. 229, 1684.)

---

* Children of James Gardner and first wife, Mary Starbuck, were Samuel, Jethro, Barnabas, Jonathan, Elizabeth, Mehitable. Patience (Folger) Gardner had no children. Rachel (Brown) Gardner had one son, James Gardner. Fourth wife, Mary(Pinkham) Gardner, had no Gardner children.

Gardner, Nathaniel, *m.* Abigail Coffin, dau. James and Mary (Severance) Coffin. (Ibid.)

Gardner, Hope, *m.* John Coffin. ("Ye Coffin Family," by Allen Coffin, LL.B., p. 56, 1692.

Gardner, Love.

CHILDREN OF JOHN GARDNER AND PRISCILLA GRAFTON.

Gardner, John, *m.* Susanna Green, of Salem. (W. C. Folger MSS., Gardner Family, p. 30.)

Gardner, Joseph. (Savage, vol. ii. p. 228.)

Gardner, Priscilla, *m.* John Arthur (second wife). (Ibid.)

Gardner, Benjamin, died young. (Ibid.)

Gardner, Rachel, *m.* 1st, John Brown; 2d, James Gardner (third wife). (Ibid.)

Gardner, Benjamin.

Gardner, George, *m.* Eunice Starbuck, dau. Nathaniel Starbuck, Sr. ("One Hundred and Sixty Allied Families," p. 220, about 1695.)

Gardner, Ann, *m.* Edward Coffin.

Gardner, Nathaniel.

Gardner, Mary, *m.* Jethro Coffin. (W. C. Folger MSS., Gardner Family, p. 30.)

Gardner, Mehitable, *m.* Ambrose Dawes, Jr. (Ibid.)

Gardner, Ruth, *m.* James Coffin, Jr. (Ibid.)

Gardner, Solomon, son Richard, Jr., *m.* Anna Coffin, dau. Stephen Coffin and Mary (Bunker). (W. C. Folger MSS., Gardner Family.)

Gardner, Paul, son Solomon, *m.* Rachel Starbuck, dau. Thomas and Rachel Starbuck. ("One Hundred and Sixty Allied Families," p. 145.)

Gardner, Paul, Jr., *m.* 1st, Sarah Mitchell, dau. Jethro Mitchell; 2d, Merab Spooner, dau. Seth and Dinah Spooner; 3d, Lydia Fitch. (W. C. Folger MSS., p. 154.)

Gardner, Zenas, son Paul and Rachel Gardner, *m.* Susanna Hussey. ("One Hundred and Sixty Allied Families," p. 145, 1790.)

Gardner, Richard[3], *m.* Leah Folger. (Nantucket Town Records, Bk. I. p. 16, 1724.)

Gardner, Miriam, dau. Richard Gardner, Jr., *m.* Samuel Coffin, son Lieutenant John Coffin. (See Coffin Family, p. 123.)

Gorham, Captain John, *m.* Desire Howland. (Plymouth Colonial Records, vol. ii. p. 79, 1644.)

Gorham, Stephen, *m.* Elizabeth Gardner (by William Worth, justice of peace). (Nantucket Town Records, Bk. I. p. 8, 1708.)

Greenleaf, Stephen, Sr., m. 1st, Elizabeth Coffin ("One Hundred and Sixty Allied Families," p. 67, 1651); 2d, Esther,* widow Captain Benjamin Swett (Ibid., p. 277, 1679).

CHILDREN OF STEPHEN GREENLEAF AND ELIZABETH COFFIN.

Greenleaf, Stephen, m. Elizabeth Gerrish, dau. William Gerrish. ("Ye Coffin Family," Allen Coffin, LL.B., p. 55, 1676.)

Greenleaf, Sarah, m. Richard Dole, of Newberry, son Richard Dole. (Ibid., 1677.)

Greenleaf, Daniel, unm. (Ibid.)

Greenleaf, Ellzabeth, m. Thomas Noyes, son James Noyes. (Ibid., 1677.)

Greenleaf, John, m. Elizabeth Hills. (Ibid., 1685.)

Greenleaf, Samuel, m. Sarah Kent, dau. John Kent. (Ibid., 1689.)

Greenleaf, Tristram, m. Margaret Piper. (Ibid., 1689.)

Greenleaf, Edmund, m. Abigail Somerby, dau. Abiel Somerby. (Ibid., 1691.)

Greenleaf, Judith, unm. (Ibid.)

Greenleaf, Mary, m. Joshua Moody, son Caleb Moody. (Ibid.)

Greenleaf, Sarah, dau. Nathaniel, and grand-dau. Tristram and Margaret (Piper) Greenleaf,† m. Joseph Whittier, 2d. (Whittier Family Records.)

Hosier, Giles, m. Elizabeth Mitchell. (Family papers, 1768.)

Hussey, John, m. Mary Wood. ("One Hundred and Sixty Allied Families," p. 142, 1598.)

Hussey, Christopher, son John Hussey, m. 1st, Theodate Batchelder (Ibid., 1632); 2d, Ann Mingay (Ibid., 1658).

CHILDREN OF CHRISTOPHER HUSSEY AND THEODATE BATCHELDER.

Hussey, Stephen, m. Martha Bunker, dau. George and Jane (Godfrey) Bunker. (W. C. Folger MSS., 1676.)

Hussey, John,‡ m. Rebecca Perkins, dau. Isaac and Susanna Perkins, of Hampton. (Savage, vol. ii. p. 507, 1659.)

---

* Esther Greenleaf, second wife of Stephen Greenleaf, Sr., died in 1718, aged eighty-nine.

† Grandparents of John Greenleaf Whittier.

‡ John Hussey, son of Christopher Hussey, had two sons and fourteen daughters. He removed after 1688 to New Castle, Dela-

Hussey, Mary, *m.* 1st, Thomas Page, son Robert and Lucy Page ("One Hundred and Sixty Allied Families," p. 143, 1664); 2d, Henry Green (Savage, vol. ii. p. 507, 1691); 3d, Henry Dow, son Henry and Joan Dow (W. C. Folger MSS., 1704.)

Hussey, Theodate.

Hussey, Huldah, *m.* John Smith, son John Smith. (Savage, vol. ii. p. 507, 1667.)

Hussey, Joseph.

CHILDREN OF STEPHEN HUSSEY AND MARTHA BUNKER.

Hussey, Puella, *m.* Stephen Gorham, son John and Mary (Otis) Gorham. ("One Hundred and Sixty Allied Families," p. 143, 1695.)

Hussey, Abigail, *m.* 1st, Thomas Hause (Nantucket Town Records, Bk. I. p. 5, 1700); 2d, Joseph Marshall, son James and Ruth (Hawkins) Marshall ("One Hundred and Sixty Allied Families," p. 143).

Hussey, Sylvanus, *m.* 1st, Abial Brown,* dau. John and Rachel (Gardner) Brown (Nantucket Town Records, Bk. I. p. 9, 1711–12); 2d, Hepzibah Starbuck, dau. Nathaniel Starbuck, Jr., and Dinah (Coffin) (Nantucket Friends' Records, Bk. I., p. 25, 1720).

Hussey, Batchelor, *m.* Abigail Hall. (Nantucket Town Records, Bk. I. p. 8, 1704.)

Hussey, Daniel, *unm.*

Hussey, Mary, *m.* 1st, Jonathan Worth, son John and Miriam (Gardner) Worth (Nantucket Town Records, Bk. I. p. 9, 1707); 2d, Ebenezer Barnard, son Nathaniel and Mary Barnard ("One Hundred and Sixty Allied Families," p. 144, 1722).

Hussey, George, *m.* Elizabeth Starbuck, dau. Nathaniel, Jr., and Dinah (Coffin) Starbuck. (Nantucket Friends' Records, Bk. I. p. 10, 1717.)

Hussey, Theodate, *m.* James Johnson. (Nantucket Town Records, Bk. I. p. 21, 1726.)

---

ware, and was a "preacher to the Quakers." (Savage, vol. ii. p. 507.)

Savage, vol. ii. pp. 507, 508, gives:

Robert Hussey, Duxbury, 1643–45; probably died 1667.

Robert Hussey, Dover, in tax-list 1659.

Robert Hussey, Boston, 1690.

* Abial Brown was great-grand-daughter of Peter Hobart. See pp. 58, 59, and Savage, vol. ii. pp. 271, 485; also History of Hingham, Massachusetts, vol. iv. p. 385.

CHILDREN OF SYLVANUS HUSSEY, SR., AND ABIAL BROWN.

Hussey, Obed, m. 1st, Margaret Wilson, dau. John and Margaret Wilson (Nantucket Town Records, Bk. I. p. 26, 1780); 2d, Mary Calef, dau. Ebenezer and Elizabeth (Fitch) Calef (Ibid., Bk. I. p. 56, 1748).

Hussey, Daniel, m. Sarah Gorham, dau. Stephen and Elizabeth (Gardner) Gorham. (Ibid., Bk. I. p. 29, 1784–85.)

Hussey, Rachel, m. 1st, Barnabas Coleman, son John and Priscilla (Starbuck) Coleman (Nantucket Friends' Records, Bk. I. p. 62, 1733); 2d, Paul Bunker, son Jabez and Hannah (Gardner) Bunker ("One Hundred and Sixty Allied Families," p. 144, 1790).

Hussey, Jonathan, m. Hepzibah Starbuck, dau. Paul and Ann (Tibbets) Starbuck. (Ibid., 1739.)

Hussey, Seth, m. Sarah Jenkins, dau. Matthew and Mary (Gardner) Jenkins. (Nantucket Friends' Records, Bk. I. p. 110, 1742.)

CHILDREN OF SYLVANUS HUSSEY, SR., AND HEPZIBAH STARBUCK.

Hussey, Christopher, m. Mary Coffin, dau. Jonathan and Hepzibah (Harker) Coffin. ("One Hundred and Sixty Allied Families," p. 145, 1743.)

Hussey, William, m. Abigail Starbuck, dau. Paul and Ann (Tibbets) Starbuck. (Nantucket Friends' Records, Bk. I. p. 52, 1746.)

Hussey, Batchelor, m. Anna Coffin, dau. Daniel and Mary (Blake) Coffin. (Ibid., p. 157, 1748.)

Hussey, Nathaniel, m. Judith Coffin, dau. Francis and Theodate (Gorham) Coffin. (Ibid., p. 185, 1750.)

Hussey, Hepzibah, m. Nathaniel Coleman, son Barnabas and Elizabeth (Barnard) Coleman. (Ibid., p. 172, 1749.)

Hussey, Sylvanus, Jr., m. 1st, Alice Gray, dau. Jeremiah and Theodate Gray ("One Hundred and Sixty Allied Families," p. 144, 1756); 2d, Lydia Wing, dau. Samuel and Hepzibah (Hathaway) Wing (Ibid.).

Hussey, George, m. Deborah Paddack, dau. Daniel and Susanna (Gorham) Paddack. (Ibid., p. 145, 1757.)

Hussey, Joseph, m. Mary Raymer. Ibid., 1766.)

CHILDREN OF GEORGE HUSSEY AND DEBORAH PADDACK.

Hussey, Rhoda, m. Tristram Folger, son Barzillai and Phebe (Coleman) Folger. ("One Hundred and Sixty Allied Families," p. 145, 1776.)

Hussey, Eunice, m. Peleg Easton, son Peleg and Mary (Frye) Easton. (Ibid., 1778.)

Hussey, George Gorham, *m.* Lydia Chase, dau. Francis and Naomi (Gardner) Chase. (Ibid.)

Hussey, Uriel, *m.* Phebe Folger, dau. William and Ruth (Coffin) Folger. (Ibid., 1789.)

Hussey, Sylvanus, *m.* Prudence Pease, dau. John and Jerusha (Norton) Pease. (Ibid., 1794.)

Hussey, Barnabas. (Ibid.)

Hussey, Susanna, *m.* Zenas Gardner, son Paul and Rachel (Starbuck) Gardner. (Ibid., 1790.)

Hussey, Deborah, *m.* Robert Brayton, son Israel and Elizabeth (Lawton) Brayton. (Ibid., 1795.)

Hussey, Alice, *unm.* (Ibid.)

Hussey, Rachel, *m.* Joseph Austin, dau. Jeremiah and Patience (Fish) Austin. (Ibid., 1808.)

Hussey, Mary, *m.* Peleg Swain. (Nantucket Town Records, Bk. I. p. 25, 1730.)

Hussey, Tristram, son Bachelor Hussey, *m.* Sarah Folger, dau. William and Ruth (Coffin) Folger. (W. C. Folger MSS., p. 171, 1777.)

Hussey, Sarah, *m.* John Milton Earle, son Pliny and Patience Earle. (Ibid., p. 180, 1821.)

Hussey, Daniel, *m.* Anna Starbuck. (Nantucket Town Records, Bk. I. p. 183, 1798.)

Hussey, Mary, *m.* Thomas Earle, son Pliny and Patience Earle. (W. C. Folger MSS., 1820.)

Hussey, Reuben, *m.* Elizabeth Woodbury. (Nantucket Town Records, Bk. I. p. 50, 1744.)

Hussey, Zaccheus, *m.* Lydia Folger. (Nantucket Court Records, Bk. I. p. 24.)

Hussey, Simeon, *m.* Abigail Bunker. (Ibid , Bk. II. p. 2, 1784.)

Hussey, Albert, *m.* Rebekah Shove. (Ibid., Bk. I. p. 28, 1785.)

Hussey, James, *m.* Eunice Swain. (Ibid., 1786.)

Hussey, Samuel, *m.* Charlotte Bartlett. (Ibid., Bk. II. p. 4, 1789.)

Hussey, Nathaniel, *m.* Elizabeth Swain. (Ibid , p. 6, 1790.)

Hussey, Ebenezer, *m.* Mehitable Smith. (Ibid., Bk. I. p. 4, 1770.)

Hussey, Reuben, *m.* Phebe Bunker. (Ibid., p. 5, 1772.)

Hussey, Jethro, *m.* Margaret Coffin. (Ibid., p. 12, 1766.)

Hussey, John, son Bachelor and Abigail, *m.* Jedidah Coffin, dau. Joseph and Bethiah Coffin. (Nantucket Friends' Records, Bk. I. p. 67, 1733–34.)

Hussey, Bethiah, *m.* Bachelor Bunker. (Nantucket Town Records, Bk. I. p. 78, 1759.)

Hussey, Abigail, *m.* Joseph Myrick. (Ibid., p. 76, 1763.)

Hussey, Hepzibah, *m.* Job Bunker. (Court Records, Bk. I. p. 29, 1767.)

Hussey, Sarah, *m.* John Darling. (Ibid., p. 1, 1767.)

Hussey, Mary, *m.* Ebenezer Perkins. (Ibid., p. 26, 1783.)

Hussey, Elizabeth, *m.* Thomas Delano. (Ibid., p. 25, 1781.)

Hussey, Lydia, *m.* Alexander Coffin. (Ibid., p. 28, 1784.)

Hussey, Susanna, *m.* Obed Barnard. (Ibid., 1786.)

Hussey, Abiel, *m.* Philip Pollard. (Ibid., p. 2, 1786.)

Hussey, Abigail, *m.* Bachelor Bunker. (Ibid., p. 14, 1778.)

DAUGHTERS OF GEORGE AND ELIZABATH (STARBUCK) HUSSEY.

Hussey, Ruth, *m.* Nathaniel Gardner, son Nathaniel and Mary Gardner. (Nantucket Friends' Records, Bk. I. p. 146, 1746.)

Hussey, Elizabeth, *m.* Peleg Coffin, son Francis and Theodate Coffin. (Ibid., p. 168, 1749.)

Hussey, Martha, *m.* Richard Swain. (son Richard and Elizabeth Swain. (Ibid., p. 197, 1751.)

Hussey, Deborah, *m.* Peter Coffin, son Paul and Mary Coffin. (Ibid., p. 87, 1738.)

Hussey, Lydia, *m.* Clothier Pierce, son Clothier and Hannah Pierce, of Newport. (Ibid., p. 113, 1742.)

Hussey, Dinah, *m.* Reuben Folger, son Jonathan and Margaret Folger. (Ibid., p. 125, 1743–44.)

Hussey, Christopher, *m.* Lydia Manchester. (Nantucket Court Records, Bk. I. p. 2, 1769.)

Hussey, Sarah, *m.* John Waterman. (Ibid., Bk. II. p. 2, 1786.)

Hussey, Abigail, *m.* Perez Waterman. (Ibid., Bk. I. p. 12, 1765.)

Hussey, Abiel, *m.* Francis Pinkham. (Ibid., p. 29, 1787.)

Hussey, Mary, *m.* Thaddeus Gardner. (Ibid., Bk. II. p. 3, 1788.)

Hussey, Elizabeth, *m.* Peter Chace. (Ibid., p. 5, 1789.)

Hussey, Abiel, *m.* Nathaniel Coffin. (Ibid., Bk. I. p. 7, 1752.)

Hussey, Elizabeth, *m.* David Basitard or Basihard. (Ibid., p. 8, 1755.)

Hussey, Lydia, *m.* Simeon Bunker. (Ibid., p. 2, 1769.)

Hussey, Margaret, *m.* Thomas Snow. (Ibid., p. 15, 1768.)

Hussey, Huldah, dau. Bachelor and Abigail Hussey, *m.* Simeon Bunker, son Jonathan and Elizabeth Bunker. (Nantucket Friends' Records, Bk. I. p. 71, 1734–35.)

Hussey, Jedidah, dau. Bachelor and Abigail Hussey, *m.* Benjamin Coffin, son Nathaniel and Damaris Coffin. (Ibid., p. 32, 1726.)

Hussey, Elizabeth, dau. Daniel and Sarah Hussey, *m.* Benjamin Coffin, son Benjamin and Jedidah Coffin. (Ibid., 1754.)

Macy[1], Thomas, *m.* Sarah Hopcot. (Macy Genealogy, p. 67.)

Macy[2], Sarah, *m.* William Worth. (Ibid., 1665.)

Macy[2], Mary, *m.* William Bunker. (Ibid., 1669.)

Macy[2], Bethiah, *m.* Joseph Gardner, son Richard and Sarah Gardner. (Ibid., 1670.)

Macy[2], John, *m.* Deborah Gardner, dau. Richard and Sarah Gardner. (Ibid.)

Macy[3], Sarah, *m.* John Barnard, son Nathaniel Barnard. (Ibid., pp. 67, 68.)

Macy[3], Deborah, *m.* Daniel Russell. (Ibid.)

Macy[3], Bethiah, *m.* 1st, Joseph Coffin, son James and Mary Coffin (Ibid., p. 68); 2d, John Renough (Ibid.).

Macy[3], Mary, *m.* Solomon Coleman, son John Coleman and Joanna (Folger). (Ibid., 1711.)

Macy[3], John,* *m.* Judith Worth, dau. John Worth and Miriam Gardner. (Ibid., pp. 67–69, 1707.)

Macy[3], Miriam, *m.* Zephaniah Coffin, son Stephen and Experience (Look) Coffin. (Ibid., 1725.)

Macy[3], Jabez, *m.* Sarah Starbuck, dau. Jethro and Dorcus Starbuck. (Ibid., p. 77, 1712.)

Macy[3], Thomas, *m.* Deborah Coffin, dau. Lieutenant John Coffin and Deborah (Austin). (Ibid., pp. 68, 78, 79.)

Macy[3], Richard,† *m.* 1st, Deborah Pinkham, dau. Richard and Mary Pinkham (Ibid., p. 68, 1711); 2d, Alice Paddack, dau. Joseph and Sarah (Gardner) Paddack (Ibid., pp. 80, 81, 1769.)

Macy[4], Anna, *m.* Joseph Jenkins, son Matthew Jenkins and Mary (Gardner). (Ibid., pp. 67–69, 1734.)

Macy[4], Judith, *m.* William Clasby, Jr., son William Clasby and Abial Gardner. (Ibid., p. 68, 1753.)

---

* John and Judith (Worth) Macy were the first of the name who joined the Society of Friends; they became members in 1711 (Macy Gen., p. 68), three years after the Society was established on the island.

† Richard Macy built the first wharf on Nantucket, in 1723, also the first windmill. (Macy Gen., p. 81.)

Note.—Figure over surname in Macy family indicates generation from Thomas Macy, proprietor and settler; five generations are here given complete.

Macy[4], Sarah, m. Richard Gardner, son Solomon and Anna (Coffin) Gardner. (Ibid., p. 68, 1746.)

Macy[4], Eunice, m. Richard Beard, son John, of Devonshire, England. (Ibid., p. 77, 1742.)

Macy[4], Lydia, m. Matthew Jenkins, son Peter and Abigail (Gardner) Jenkins. (Ibid., 1758.)

Macy[4], Love, m. Joseph Rotch, son William and Hannah Rotch. (Ibid., pp. 68, 78, 79, 1783.)

Macy[4], Lydia, m. Jethro Coleman, son John and Priscilla (Starbuck) Coleman. (Ibid., 1747.)

Macy[4], Elizabeth, m. Francis Barnard, son Benj. and Judith (Gardner) Barnard. (Ibid., p. 78, 1741.)

Macy[4], Deborah, m. Benjamin Coffin, son Nathaniel and Damaris (Gayer) Coffin. (Ibid.)

Macy[4], Anna, m. Richard Worth, son Richard and Sarah (Hoag) Worth. (Ibid., 1752.)

Macy[4], Hepzibeth, m. Thomas Davis. (Ibid., 1752.)

Macy[4], Mary, m. Benjamin Marshall. (Macy Genealogy, p. 81, 1749.)

Macy[4], Judith, m. Jonathan Bunker, son Peleg Bunker and Susanna (Coffin). (Ibid., 1742.)

Macy[4], Ruth, m. Joseph Starbuck, son Paul Starbuck and Ann (Tibbets). (Ibid., 1744.)

Macy[4], David, m. Dinah Gardner, dau. Solomon Gardner and Anna (Coffin). (Ibid., p. 82, 1739.)

Macy[4], John, m. Eunice Coleman, dau. Elihu and Jemima (Barnard) Coleman. (Ibid., p. 84, 1743.)

Macy[4], Jonathan, son John, m. Lois Gorham, dau. Stephen and Elizabeth (Gardner) Gorham. (Ibid., p. 85, 1744.)

Macy[4], William, m. Mary Barney, dau. Benj. and Lydia (Starbuck) Barney. (Ibid., p. 86, 1746.)

Macy[4], Jethro, m. Hepzibeth Worth, dau. William and Mary (Butler) Worth. (Ibid., p. 87, 1750.)

Macy[4], Daniel, son Jabez, m. Abigail Swain, dau. Caleb and Margaret (Paddack) Swain. (Ibid., p. 88, 1755.)

Macy[4], Matthew, m. 1st, Abigail Coffin, dau. Benj. and Jedidah (Hussey) Coffin (Ibid., p. 89, 1755); 2d, Abigail Gardner, dau. Barnabas and Mary (Wheeler) Gardner (Ibid., 1761).

Macy[4], Jabez, m. Rachel Cartwright, dau. Hezidiah and Abigail (Brown) Cartwright. (Ibid., 1767.)

Macy[4], Joseph, m. Hannah Hobbs, dau. Benjamin Hobbs. (Ibid., p. 90, 1728.)

Macy[4], Robert, *m.* Abigail Barnard, dau. Benjamin and Judith (Gardner) Barnard. (Ibid., p. 94, 1731.)

Macy[4], Francis, *m.* Judith Coffin, dau. Richard and Ruth (Coffin) Bunker. (Ibid., 1788.)

Macy[4], Nathaniel, *m.* Abigail Pinkham, dau. Shubael and Abigail (Bunker) Pinkham. (Ibid., p. 95, 1741.)

Macy[4], Zaccheus, *m.* Hepzibah Gardner, dau. Samuel and Patience (Swain) Gardner. (Ibid., p. 96, 1784.)

Macy[4], Abraham, *m.* Anna Worth, dau. Joseph and Lydia (Gorham) Worth. (Ibid., p. 109, 1788.)

Macy[4], Caleb, *m.* Judith Gardner (widow James), dau. Daniel and Abigail Folger. (Ibid., p. 110, 1749.)

Macy[4], Benjamin, *m.* Abigail Brown, dau. George and Abigail (Trott) Brown. (Ibid., p. 111.)

Macy[5], Miriam, dau. David, *m.* Robert Gardner, son Robert and Jedidah Gardner. (Ibid., p. 82, 1761.)

Macy[5], Anna, *m.* Enoch Macy, son Joseph and Hannah (Hobbs) Macy. (Ibid., 1768.)

Macy[5], Sarah, *m.* Timothy Russell, son William and Ruth (Swain) Russell. (Ibid., 1766.)

Macy[5], Bethiah, *m.* Paul Macy, son Joseph and Hannah (Hobbs) Macy. (Ibid., p. 84, 1761.)

Macy[5], Judith, *m.* Reuben Bunker, son Reuben and Mary (Chase) Bunker. (Ibid., 1762.)

Macy[5], Jemima, *m.* Barzillai Gardner, son Stephen and Jemima (Worth) Gardner. (Ibid.)

Macy[5], Merab, *m.* Timothy Macy, son Jethro and Hepzibah (Worth) Macy. (Ibid., 1783.)

Macy[5], Amy, *m.* Libni Barnard, son Benj. and Eunice (Fitch) Barnard. (Ibid.)

Macy[5], Abigail, dau. John, *m.* Benjamin Stanton, son Benjamin and Lydia (Albison) Stanton, of North Carolina. (Ibid., p. 88, 1744.)

Macy[5], Elizabeth, *m.* Elihu Coleman, son Jethro and Lydia (Paddack) Coleman. (Ibid., p. 85, 1762.)

Macy[5], Hepzibeth, *m.* Thomas Pierce. (Ibid., p. 87.)

Macy[5], Mary, *m.* Samuel Coffin, son William and Priscilla (Paddack) Coffin. (Ibid.)

Macy[5], Jedidah, *m.* Joseph Swain, son Nathaniel and Bethiah (Macy) Swain. (Ibid.)

Macy[5], Huldah, *m.* Asa Barnard, son Tristram and Margaret (Folger) Barnard. (Ibid., p. 88, 1792.)

Macy[5], Margaret, *m.* Obed Paddack, son Jonathan and Keziah (Gardner) Paddack. (Ibid., p. 88, 1787.)

Macy[5], Abigail, dau. Daniel, *m.* Matthew Barney, son Benjamin and Jemima (Jackson) Barney. (Ibid., 1791.)

Macy[5], Sarah, *m.* Stephen Springer. (Ibid., p. 89.)

Macy[5], Abigail, dau. Matthew, *m.* Joseph Coffin, son Peter and Priscilla (Coleman) Coffin. (Ibid.)

Macy[5], Elizabeth, *m.* Libni Coffin, son Libni and Hepzibah (Starbuck) Coffin. (Ibid.)

Macy[5], Lydia, dau. Jabez, *m.* Uriah Starbuck, son Sylvanus and Mary (Howes) Starbuck. (Ibid., 1786.)

Macy[5], Mary, *m.* 1st, Paul Way, son John and Mary (Long) Way (Ibid., p. 90, 1753); 2d, James Anthony (Ibid., 1776).

Macy[5], Bethiah, *m.* Nathaniel Swain, son Caleb and Margaret (Paddack) Swain. (Ibid., 1755.)

Macy[5], Lydia, dau. Robert, *m.* Abishai Gardner, son Robert and Jedidah (Folger) Gardner. (Ibid., p. 94, 1751.)

Macy[5], Elizabeth, *m.* 1st, Alexander Mooers, son Thomas and Mary (Stratton) Mooers (Ibid., 1762); 2d, William Coffin (his third wife), son Benj. and Jedidah (Hussey) Coffin (Ibid.).

Macy[5], Judith, *m.* Benjamin Stratton, son Caleb and Lois (Oder) Stratton. (Ibid., p. 93, 1758.)

Macy[5], Deborah, *m.* Jonathan Cartwright, son Hezidiah and Abigail (Brown) Cartwright. (Ibid., 1769.)

Macy[5], Abigail, dau. Robert, *m.* Thomas Butts. (Ibid., p. 93.)

Macy[3], Eunice, dau. Robert, *m.* Francis Bunker, son Shubael and Lydia (Paddack) Bunker. (Ibid.)

Macy[5], Love, *m.* James Cartwright, son Hezidiah and Abigail (Brown) Cartwright. (Ibid., p. 94, 1758.)

Macy[5], Phebe, *m.* Benjamin Hussey, son John and Jedidah (Coffin) Hussey. (Ibid., 1763.)

Macy[5], Judith, *m.* Benjamin Coffin, son Benjamin and Rebecca (Coffin) Coffin. (Ibid., 1772.)

Macy[5], Anna, *m.* Tristram Jenkins, son Peter and Abigail (Gardner) Jenkins. (Ibid., 1774.)

Macy[5], Ruth, *m.* Obadiah Folger, son Barzillai and Phebe (Coleman) Folger. (Ibid., 1755.)

Macy[5], Lydia, dau. Francis, *m.* Edward Starbuck, son Edward and Damaris (Worth) Starbuck. (Ibid., 1784.)

Macy[5], Eunice, dau. Nathaniel, *m.* Solomon Coffin, son Zephaniah and Abigail (Coleman) Coffin. (Ibid., p. 95.)

Macy[5], Phebe, *m.* 1st, Paul Barnard, son William and Mary

(Coffin) Barnard (Ibid., 1778); 2d, Paul Worth, son John and Mary (Gardner) Worth (Ibid.).

Macy[5], Elizabeth, dau. Nathaniel, m. Barzilai Macy, son Caleb and Judith (Gardner) Macy. (Ibid., 1787.)

Macy[5], Mary, dau. Zaccheus, m. John Ray, son Samuel and Mary (Fullerton or Fullington) Ray. (Ibid., p. 96, 1758.)

Macy[5], Hannah, m. Reuben Swain, son Stephen and Eleanor (Ellis) Swain. (Ibid., 1756.)

Macy[5], Phebe, dau. Zaccheus, m. William Stanton, son Samuel and Sarah (Coffin) Stanton. (Ibid., 1756.)

Macy[5], Hepzibah, dau. Zaccheus, m. Nathaniel Macy, son Robert and Abigail (Barnard) Macy. (Ibid.)

Macy[5], Priscilla, m. Enoch Ray, son Samuel and Mary Ray. (Ibid.)

Macy[5], Ruth, dau. Zaccheus, m. Thomas Barnard, son Thomas and Sarah (Hoag) Barnard. (Ibid., 1768.)

Macy[5], Deborah, dau. Zaccheus, m. Daniel Ray, son Samuel and Elizabeth (Coleman) Ray. (Ibid.)

Macy[5], Anna, dau. Abraham, m. Edward Allen, son Ebenezer and Christiana (Heath) Allen. (Ibid., p. 109, 1761.)

Macy[5], Ruth, dau. Abraham, m. Job Chase, son Benjamin and Martha Chase. (Ibid., p. 110, 1796.)

Macy[5], John,* m. 1st, Bethiah Cartwright, dau. Hezidiah and Abigail (Brown) Cartwright (Ibid., pp. 136, 137, 1768); 2d, Phebe Macy (Ibid., 1794).

Mitchell[1], Richard, m. Mary Wood. (W. C. Folger MSS. and Mitchell Family Records.)

Mitchell[2], Richard, m. Elizabeth Tripp, dau. James Tripp.† (Ibid., 1708.)

---

* John Macy, of the fifth generation from Thomas Macy[1], signed his last will when he was eighty-eight years old, and had nineteen children. The Macy family was a close corporation for many years. Up to 1800 very few surnames appear, excepting such as may be classed among orthodox Nantucket names. Upon these many changes were rung. Since that date record of intermarriages with many other families may be found. Among these are Willis, Howland, Havens, Knowles, Watson, Dingman, Wilcox, Foster, Baldwin, etc.

† James Tripp was son of John, of Aquidneck, Rhode Island. John Tripp was admitted an inhabitant, 1638; commissioner, 1655; assistant, 1670–73–74–75; also member of Town Council for many years.

Mitchell[3], Richard, *m.* Mary Starbuck. (Nantucket Friends' Records, Bk. I. p. 54, 1731.)

Mitchell[4], Richard, *m.* Hepzibah Barnard, dau. Robert Barnard. (Ibid., p. 223, 1755.)

Mitchell[4], Peleg, Sr., *m.* Lydia Cartwright. (Nantucket Friends' Records, Bk. II. 1779.)

CHILDREN OF PELEG MITCHELL, SR., AND LYDIA CARTWRIGHT.

Mitchell, George, *m.* 1st, Phebe Chase (Nantucket Friends' Records, Bk. II. p. 429, 1807); 2d, Susan Barnard (Ibid., Bk. III., p. 88, 1834).

Mitchell, William, *m.* Lydia Coleman. (Ibid., Bk. II., p. 452, 1812.)

Mitchell, Hannah, *m.* Reuben Macy. (Nantucket Friends' Records, 1816.)

Mitchell, Lydia, *m.* Richard Mitchell, of Rhode Island. (Ibid., Bk. III. p. 2, 1818.)

Mitchell, Peleg, Jr., *m.* Mary S. Russell. (Nantucket Friends' Records, 1837.)

Mitchell, Love, *m.* Isaac Brayton. (Ibid., Bk. III. p. 19, 1825.)

Mitchell, John R., *m.* Eliza Brock. (W. C. Folger MSS., Mitchell Family, p. 135.)

Mitchell, John, *m.* Meriba Mitchell. (Ibid.)

Mitchell, Paul, *m.* Merab Coffin, dau. Alexander and Eunice (Bunker) Coffin. (Ibid., p. 132.)

Mitchell, James, *m.* Ann Folger, dau. Jethro Folger and Mary (Starbuck). (Nantucket Friends' Records, Bk. I. p. 86, 1738.)

Newhall, Estes, *m.* Hepzibah Wing. (Sandwich Friends' Records, 1798.)

Newhall, Paul Wing, *m.* Hannah Johnson, dau. Samuel and Sarah Johnson. (Newhall Family Records, 1831.)

Paddack, Zechariah, *m.* Deborah Sears. ("One Hundred and Sixty Allied Families," p. 188, 1659.)

Paddack, Nathaniel, *m.* Ann Bunker. (Ibid., 1706.)

CHILDREN OF NATHANIEL PADDACK.

Paddack, Deborah, *m.* Theophilus Pinkham. ("One Hundred and Sixty Allied Families," p. 188, 1728.)

Paddack, Love, *m.* George Swain. (Ibid., 1729.)

Paddack, Lydia, *m.* Jethro Coleman. (Ibid., 1731.)

Paddack, Paul, *m.* Ann Coffin. (Ibid., 1740.)

Paddack, Mary, *m.* Francis Swain. (Ibid., 1786.)

Paddack, Dinah, *m.* Christopher Worth. (Ibid., 1738.)

Paddack, Priscilla, *m.* William Coffin. (Ibid., 1740.)

Paddack, Daniel, *m.* Susanna Gorham. (Ibid, 1726.)

Paddack, Elizabeth, *m.* Joseph Swain. (Ibid., 1746.)

Paddack, Stephen, *m.* Eunice Coffin. (Ibid., 1751.)

Puddack, Lydia, *m.* Shubael Bunker. (Ibid., p. 189, 1750.)

Paddack, Susanna, *m.* 1st, Matthew Gardner (Ibid., 1752); 2d, George Freeborn (Ibid., 1767).

Paddack, Eunice, *m.* 1st, Joseph Coffin (Ibid., 1775); 2d, Robert Clasby (Ibid.).

Paddack, Deborah, *m.* George Hussey. (Ibid., 1757.)

Paddack, Barnabas, *m.* Abigail Gardner. (Ibid., 1764)

Paddack, Daniel, *m.* Susanna Gorham. (Nantucket Friends' Records, Bk. I. p. 38, 1726.)

Paddack, Nathaniel, *m.* Deborah Pinkham (by "Bezaleel Shaw, Minister of the Gospel"). (Nantucket Court Records, Bk. I. p. 25, 1782.)

Pinkham, Reuben, *m.* Anna Starbuck (by Jeremiah Gardner, justice of peace). (Nantucket Town Records, Bk. I. p. 68, 1755.)

Prence, Thomas, *m.* 1st, Patience Brewster, dau. Elder Brewster (1624); 2d, Mary Collier, dau. William Collier (Winsor's History of Duxbury, p. 248, 1635); 3d, —— Freeman, widow Samuel Freeman (Plymouth Colonial Records, vol. i. p. 34, 1662).

Rodman, Joseph, *m.* Mary Miller. (Gen. of Rodman Family, p. 27, 1745.)

Rodman, Hannah, dau. Joseph, *m.* William Mitchell, son Richard and Mary (Starbuck) Mitchell. (Ibid., 1767.)

Rodman, Clark, son Joseph, *m.* Abigail Lawton. (Ibid., p. 89, 1775.)

Rodman, David, *m.* Joanna Mitchell. (Ibid.)

Rodman, Thomas, *m.* Mary Borden. (Ibid., p. 27, 1750.)

Rodman, Elizabeth, dau. Thomas, *m.* William Rotch, Jr. (Ibid., p. 41, 1782.)

Rodman, Samuel, son Thomas and Mary, *m.* Elizabeth Rotch. (Ibid., p. 89, 1780.)

Rodman, Anna, *m.* Thomas Hazzard. (Ibid., p. 32, 1780.)

Rotch, Joseph, son William and Hannah Rotch, *m.* Love Macy, dau. Thomas and Deborah (Coffin) Macy. (Nantucket Friends' Records, Bk. I. p. 69, 1733.)

Rotch, William, son Joseph and Love (Macy) Rotch, m. Elizabeth Barney, dau. Benjamin and Lydia (Starbuck) Barney. (Ibid., p. 229, 1754.)

Rotch, Sarah, m. James Arnold. (Gen. of Rodman Family, p. 72, 1807.)

Russell[1], Daniel, m. Deborah Macy. (Macy Genealogy, pp. 67, 68.)

Russell[2], John, 1st, m. Ruth Starbuck. (Nantucket Friends' Records, Bk. I. p. 60, 1731-32.)

Russell[3], John, 2d, m. Hepzibah Coleman. (Ibid., 1777.)

Russell[4], Barnabas, m. Mary Swain. (Ibid., 1811.)

Russell[2], Jonathan, m. Patience Swain. (W. C. Folger MSS.)

Russell, Sylvanus, m. Anna Coffin. (Ibid.)

Russell, Uriah, m. Lydia Swain. (Ibid.)

Sears, Richard, m. Dorothy Thatcher. ("One Hundred and Sixty Allied Families," pp. 205, 240, 1632.)

Stanton, Samuel, son John and Elizabeth Stanton, m. Sarah Coffin, dau. Samuel and Miriam Coffin. (Nantucket Friends' Records, Bk. I. p. 68, 1733-34.)

Stanton, Giles E., m. Hannah Beebe. (Nantucket Town Records, Bk. I. p. 163, 1805.)

Stanton, Benjamin, m. Abigail Macy. (See Macy Family, p. 83, 1774.)

Starbuck, Edward, m. Katharine Reynolds. (N. E. Hist. and Gen. Reg., vol. viii. p. 68.)

CHILDREN OF EDWARD STARBUCK AND KATHARINE REYNOLDS.

Starbuck, Nathaniel, m. Mary Coffin. (See Coffin Family, p. 122.)

Starbuck, Jethro, unm.

Starbuck, Sarah, m. 1st, William Story, d. 1658 (N. E. Hist. and Gen. Reg., vol. viii. p. 129, 1658); 2d, Joseph Austin, d. 1663 (W. C. Folger MSS., 1664); 3d, Humphrey Varney,* as second wife (1664).

Starbuck, Dorcas, m. William Gayer. (W. C. Folger, MSS.)

Starbuck, Abigail, m. Peter Coffin. (See Coffin Family, p. 122.)

Starbuck, Esther, m. Humphrey Varney. (W. C. Folger MSS.)

CHILDREN OF NATHANIEL STARBUCK, SR., AND MARY COFFIN.

Starbuck, Mary, m. James Gardner, son Richard Gardner. ("Ye Coffin Family," by Allen Coffin, LL.B., pp. 57, 58.)

---

* Humphrey Varney's first wife was Esther, sister of Sarah Starbuck.

Starbuck, Elizabeth, *m.* 1st, Peter Coffin, Jr. (N. E. Hist. and Gen. Reg., 1682); 2d, Nathaniel Barnard, Jr. ("One Hundred and Sixty Allied Families," p. 220).

Starbuck, Nathaniel, Jr., *m.* Dinah Coffin. (See Coffin Family, p. 128, 1690.)

Starbuck, Jethro, *m.* Dorcas Gayer. (Nantucket Town Records, Bk. I. p. 7, 1694.)

Starbuck, Eunice, *m.* George Gardner, son John Gardner. (See Gardner Family, p. 130, W. C. Folger MSS.)

Starbuck, Priscilla, *m.* John Coleman, 2d, grandson Thomas Coleman[1]. (See Coleman Family, p. 125, Ibid.)

Starbuck, Hepzibah, *m.* Thomas Hathaway, of Dartmouth, Massachusetts. ("One Hundred and Sixty Allied Families," p. 220, about 1697.)

CHILDREN OF NATHANIEL STARBUCK, JR., AND DINAH COFFIN.

Starbuck, Mary, *m.* Jethro Folger. ("One Hundred and Sixty Allied Families," p. 221, 1709.)

Starbuck, Paul, *m.* 1st, Ann Tibbets (Ibid., 1718); 2d, Keziah Gardner, widow Jethro (Ibid.); 3d, Elizabeth Coffin, widow Daniel (Ibid., 1751).

Starbuck, Priscilla, *m.* Shubael Coffin. (Ibid., 1717.)

Starbuck, Elizabeth, *m.* George Hussey. (Ibid., 1717.)

Starbuck, Hepzibah, *m.* Sylvanus Hussey, Sr. (See Hussey Family, pp. 132, 188, W. C. Folger MSS., 1728.)

Starbuck, Abigail, *m.* 1st, Thomas Howey ("One Hundred and Sixty Allied Families," p. 221, 1723); 2d, John Way (Ibid., 1741).

Starbuck, Benjamin, *m.* Dinah Coffin, dau. Stephen Coffin, Jr. (Ibid., 1730.)

Starbuck, Tristram, son Nathaniel, Jr., and Dinah (Coffin) Starbuck, *m.* Deborah Coffin, dau. Samuel and Miriam Coffin. (Nantucket Friends' Records, Bk. I. p. 49, 1729.)

Starbuck, Ruth, *m.* John Russell. (Ibid., p. 60, 1731-32.)

Starbuck, Anna, *m.* Peter Barnard. ("One hundred and Sixty Allied Families," p. 221, 1733.)

Swain, Richard, *m.* 1st, Elizabeth ——; 2d, Jane (Godfrey) Bunker, widow George Bunker. (Nantucket Town Records, 1662.)

CHILDREN OF RICHARD SWAIN AND FIRST WIFE.

Swain, Francis, *m.* Martha ——. (W. C. Folger MSS., p. 61.)

Swain, William, of Hampton, New Hampshire, *m.* Prudence ——. (Ibid.)

Swain, Dorothy, *m.* 1st, Thomas Abbott; 2d, Edward Chapman. (Ibid.)

Swain, Elizabeth, *m.* Nathaniel Weare. (N. E. Hist. and Gen. Reg., vol. xxv. p. 246, 1656.)

Swain, John, *m.* Mary Wier or Weare. ("One Hundred and Sixty Allied Families," p. 227.)

CHILD OF RICHARD AND SECOND WIFE.

Swain, Richard.

Swain, John, 2d, *m.* Experience Folger. (See Folger Family, p. 126.)

Swain, John, 3d, *m.* 1st, Patience Swift (Nantucket Town Records, Bk. I. p. 6, 1706); 2d, Mary Swett, dau. Benjamin and Hester (Weare) Swett (Ibid., p. 9, 1711–12).

Swain, Francis, 1st, *m.* Mary Paddack. (See Paddack Family, p. 142, 1786.)

Swain, Francis, 2d, *m.* Lydia Barker. (Nantucket Friends' Records, 1767.)

Swain, Elizabeth, *m.* Benjamin Swift. (Nantucket Town Records, Bk. I. p. 129, 1791.)

Swain, Joseph, *m.* Phebe Barney, dau. Benjamin and Huldah Barney. (W. C. Folger MSS.)

Swift, Dr. Paul, *m.* Dorcas Gardner. (W. C. Folger MSS., p. 164, 1827.)

Trip, John, *m.* Mary Paine, dau. Anthony Paine. (Austin's R. I. Gen. Dict.)

Wier, Hester, *m.* 1st, Benjamin Swett ("One Hundred and Sixty Allied Families," p. 277, 1647); 2d, Stephen Greenleaf, Sr. (Ibid., 1679).

Wing, Samuel, *m.* Hepzibah Hathaway. (Ibid., p. 144.)

Wing, John, Sandwich, *m.* Deborah Batchelder, dau. Rev. Stephen Batchelder. (Ibid., p. 272.)

Note.—Francis Swain went to Long Island; William remained at Hampton, New Hampshire; Richard, the only child of second wife, Jane, removed to New Jersey, and has many descendants there.

Wing, Paul, *m.* Abigail Wing. (Sandwich Friends Records, 1768.)

Wing, Zaccheus, *m.* Content Swift. (Ibid., 1731.)

Note.—In recorded dates we often find two years given,—*i.e.*, 1637–38. In what was known as old style, the year began March 25, and when the new or present style was adopted many were not pleased with the innovation; recorders therefore accommodated themselves to the caprice of the people, and gave the date in accordance with both methods. This will account for any discrepancy covering not more than three months.

Note.—William C. Folger, whose MSS. are here quoted, was Corresponding Member of the New England Genealogical Society, and prepared a number of Nantucket Genealogical notes for Savage.

ERRATA.

On pages 90 and 92, in place of Sarah (Mayhew) *read* Dinah Starbuck (widow Benjamin Starbuck and daughter Stephen Coffin, Jr., and Experience (Look) Coffin).

Also on page 92, *omit* Thomas Mayhew, Sr., and Thomas Mayhew, Jr., from list of ancestors.

On page 141, seventeenth line from bottom, instead of Mitchell, John, *m.* Meriba Mitchell, *read* Brock, John, *m.* Meriba Mitchell.

INDEX.

Alden Family, 93.
Allen, Ann (Mrs. Edward Allen, dau. Joseph Coleman), 102.
Allen, Edward, 102.
Allen Family, 93.
Allen, Rachel (Mrs. Thomas Starbuck, dau. Edward Allen), 101, 102.
Andros, Edmund, Governor, 71.
Austin, Abigail (Mrs. Richard Austin), 39.
Austin, Deborah (Mrs. John Coffin, dau. Joseph Austin), 30, 85, 86, 95, 105, 112, 113.
Austin, Joseph, 30, 39, 86, 95, 101, 105, 113, 117.
Austin, Mary (Mrs. Richard Gardner, 2d, dau. Joseph Austin), 100, 101, 113, 116, 117.
Austin, Richard, 39.
Austin, Sarah (Mrs. Joseph Austin, dau. Edward Starbuck), 22, 30, 86, 95, 101, 105, 113, 117.

Bache, Richard, 49.
Bache, Sarah (Mrs. Richard Bache), 49.
Bachiler. See Batchilder.
Balch, Anice (Mrs. John Balch), 98.
Balch, Benjamin, 98.
Balch, John, 98.
Balch, Ruth (Mrs. John Drinker, dau. Benjamin Balch), 97, 98.
Balch, Sarah (Mrs. Benjamin Balch), 98.
Barker, Abraham, 90.
Barker, Bethiah (Mrs. Samuel Barker), 52, 90.
Barker, Elizabeth (Mrs. Isaac Barker), 115.
Barker Family, 52, 90, 92, 115.
Barker, Francis, 90.
Barker, Isaac, 52, 90, 115.
Barker, Jacob, 52, 54, 90, 106.
Barker, James, 90.
Barker, Jedidah (Mrs. Robert Barker), 90, 92.
Barker, Jedidah (dau. Robert Barker), 90.

Barker, Judith (dau. Robert Barker), 52, 90.
Barker, Judith (Mrs. Isaac Barker, 1st), 90, 115.
Barker, Lydia (Mrs. Francis Swain, Jr., dau. Robert Barker), 90, 93.
Barker, Margaret (dau. Robert Barker), 90.
Barker, Mary (dau. Robert Barker), 90.
Barker, Prince, 115.
Barker, Robert, 52, 54, 90, 92, 106.
Barker, Samuel, 52, 90.
Barker, Sarah (Mrs. Robert Barker, widow Hezikiah Gardner, dau. Abishai Folger), 52, 90, 92.
Barker, Sarah (dau. Robert Barker), 90.
Barkers, Nantucket, 115.
Barnard or Bernard, Bethiah (Mrs. John Barnard), 45.
Barnard, Eleanor (Mrs. Thomas Barnard), 45, 91, 114.
Barnard Family, 45.
Barnard, Joanna (Mrs. Robert Barnard), 45, 91, 115.
Barnard, John, 45.
Barnard, Mary[1] (Mrs. Nathaniel Barnard, dau. Robert Barnard), 45, 91, 114, 115.
Barnard, Mary[2] (Mrs. John Folger, dau. Nathaniel Barnard), 90, 91, 114.
Barnard motto on coat of arms, 45.
Barnard, Nathaniel, 45, 91, 114.
Barnard, Reuben, 45.
Barnard, Robert, 13, 15, 45, 48, 91, 92, 94, 115.
Barnard, Thomas, 10, 11, 13, 45, 91, 92, 94, 114, 115.
Barnes, Elizabeth (Mrs. Nathaniel Coffin, dau. Henry Barnes), 34.
Barnes, Henry, 34.
Barney, Benjamin, 105.
Barney, Elizabeth (Mrs. William Rotch), 104, 105, 106.
Barney, Lydia (Mrs. Benjamin Barney), 105.

Batchilder or Bachiler, Abigail (Mrs. Richard Austin), 39.

Batchilder, Deborah (Mrs. Nathaniel Batchilder), 39.

Batchilder, Deborah (Mrs. John Wing, dau. Rev. Stephen Batchilder), 38, 110.

Batchilder, Francis, 39.

Batchilder, Mary (Mrs. Nathaniel Batchilder), 39.

Batchilder, Nathaniel, 39.

Batchilder, Rev. Stephen, 37, 38, 39, 89, 99, 100, 102, 103, 109, 110, 111.

Batchilder, Theodate (Mrs. Christopher Hussey, dau. Rev. Stephen Batchilder), 37, 38, 88, 89, 99, 101, 102, 108, 109, 110.

Bates, James, 74.

Beebe, Hannah (Mrs. Giles E. Stanton), 117.

Biron or Bjorne, 7.

Bishop, John, 13.

Bon Cœur, 109.

Bradford, Jael (Mrs. Joseph Bradford, dau. Peter Hobart), 59.

Bradford, Joseph, 59.

Brayton, Judge, 86.

Brayton, Love (Mrs. Judge Brayton), 86.

Brewster, Love, 52.

Brewster, Sarah (Mrs. Love Brewster, dau. William Collier), 52.

Brown, Abial (Mrs. Sylvanus Hussey, dau. John Brown, Jr.), 88, 89.

Brown, Abigail (Mrs. Hezidiah Cartwright), 84.

Brown, Hannah (Mrs. John Brown, of Salem), 58, 59, 89, 91.

Brown, John, Elder, 41, 58, 89, 91.

Brown, John, of Salem, 58, 59, 89, 91.

Brown, Rachel (Mrs. John Brown), 58, 89, 91.

Brown, Rachel (Mrs. James Chase, dau. John Brown), 91.

Buffum Connection, 114.

Buffum, David, 114, 115.

Buffum Family, 115.

Buffum, Hepzibah (Mrs. David Buffum), 114, 115.

Buffum, Joshua, 62, 63.

Bunker, Ann (Mrs. Joseph Coleman), 102.

Bunker, Ann (Mrs. Nathaniel Paddack, dau. William Bunker), 93, 103, 108, 109.

Bunker, Desire (Mrs. Zachariah Bunker), 107.

Bunker, Elizabeth (Mrs. Jonathan Bunker), 85, 96, 108.

Bunker, Elizabeth (Mrs. Nathan Bunker, 2d), 107, 109.

Bunker Family, 107.

Bunker, George, 31, 46, 109.

Bunker, Hepsibeth (Mrs. Nathan Bunker), 107.

Bunker, Jane (Mrs. George Bunker), 31, 109.

Bunker, Jane (Mrs. Richard Swain, widow George Bunker), 46.

Bunker, Jonathan, 85, 96, 108.

Bunker, Lydia (Mrs. Shubael Bunker), 107.

Bunker, Martha (Mrs. Stephen Hussey), 38, 88, 98, 101, 108, 110.

Bunker, Mary (Mrs. Stephen Coffin, dau. George Bunker), 31, 101, 116.

Bunker, Mary (Mrs. William Bunker), 85, 93, 96, 103, 108, 109.

Bunker, Mary Clement, 109.

Bunker, Nathan, Jr., 107, 109.

Bunker, Nathan, Sr., 107.

Bunker, Priscilla, 29.

Bunker, Ruth (Mrs. Richard Coffin), 85, 95, 96.

Bunker, Shubael, 107.

Bunker, William, 85, 93, 96, 103, 108, 109.

Bunker, Zachariah, 107, 108.

Burroughs, Edward, 64, 66.

Butler Family, 93.

Butler, William Allen, 54.

Cartwright, Abigail (Mrs. Hezidiah Cartwright), 84.

Cartwright, Bethiah (Mrs. Sampson Cartwright), 84.

Cartwright, Hezidiah, 84.

Cartwright, James, 84.

Cartwright, Lydia (Mrs. Peleg Mitchell, Sr., dau. James Cartwright), 83, 84, 86, 87.

Cartwright, Love (Mrs. James Cartwright), 84.

Cartwright, Sampson, 84.

Chase, Isaac, Lieutenant, 91, 92, 94.

Chase, James, 91.

Chase, Jedidah (Mrs. Robert Barker, dau. James Chase), 90, 91, 92.

Chase, Mary (Mrs. Lieutenant Isaac Chase), 91.

Chase, Rachel (Mrs. James Chase), 91.

Christisen, Wenlock, 67.

Church, Sarah (Mrs. Nathan Folger), 95.

Clement, Elizabeth Thorne (Mrs. Nathan Bunker), 107, 109.

Coffin, Abigail (dau. Edward Starbuck), 22, 27.

Coffin, Anna (Mrs. Thomas Coffin), 94, 97.

Coffin, Anna (Mrs. Solomon Gardner, dau. Stephen Coffin), 100, 101, 116.

Coffin, Benjamin, 94.

Coffin, Damaris (Mrs. Nathaniel Coffin), 94.

Coffin, Deborah (Mrs. Benjamin Coffin), 94.

Coffin, Deborah (Mrs. Tristram Starbuck, dau. Samuel Coffin), 112.

Coffin, Deborah (Mrs. Lieutenant John Coffin, dau. Joseph Austin), 30, 85, 95, 105, 112.

Coffin, Deborah (dau. Tristram Coffin. Died in infancy), 28.

Coffin, Deborah (Mrs. Thomas Macy², dau. Lieutenant John Coffin), 84, 85, 94, 95, 105.

Coffin, Dinah (Mrs. Nathaniel Starbuck, Jr., dau. James Coffin), 87, 88, 99, 102, 103, 110, 112, 113, 114.

Coffin, Dionis (Mrs. Tristram Coffin, Sr.), 24, 40, 43, 84, 85, 88, 89, 94, 95, 96, 97, 99, 101, 102, 103, 105, 108, 109, 110, 111, 112, 113, 114, 115, 116.

Coffin, Eliza (Mrs. Benjamin H. Yarnall), 97.

Coffin, Elizabeth (Mrs. Captain Stephen Greenleaf, dau. Tristram Coffin, Sr.), 28, 40, 43.

Coffin, Elizabeth (Mrs. Jonathan Bunker, 2d), 85, 86, 96, 108.

Coffin, Elizabeth (Mrs. Nathaniel Coffin, dau. Henry Barnes), 34.

Coffin, Elizabeth (Mrs. Sir Isaac Coffin, dau. T. Greenly, Esq.), 34, 35.

Coffin, Hope (Mrs. John Coffin, Esq.), 85, 95.

Coffin, Isaac, Sir, 33, 34, 35, 36.

Coffin, James, 13, 15, 19, 28, 30, 31, 34, 85, 86, 88, 89, 92, 94, 96, 97, 99, 100, 103, 108, 109, 110, 111, 113, 114, 115.

Coffin, Joan (mother Tristram Coffin, Sr.), 24.

Coffin, John (died in infancy. Son Tristram Coffin), 28.

Coffin, John, Esq., 96, 97.

Coffin, John, Lieutenant, 30, 31, 33, 85, 86, 95, 97, 105, 107, 112, 113.

Coffin, Joseph, 32.

Coffin, Joshua, 32, 38, 43.

Coffin, Judith (Mrs. Francis Macy, dau. Richard Coffin), 84, 85.

Coffin, Judith (Mrs. Tristram Coffin, Jr., dau. Edmund Greenleaf), 27.

Coffin, Lucretia (Mrs. James Mott, dau. Thomas Coffin), 97.

Coffin, Margaret (Mrs. Joseph Coffin, dau. Benjamin Morse), 32.

Coffin, Martha (Mrs. Peter Pelham, dau. Thomas Coffin), 98.

Coffin, Mary (Mrs. Nathaniel Starbuck, Sr., dau. Tristram Coffin, Sr.), 23, 28, 29, 84, 87, 88, 89, 99, 101, 102, 103, 105, 109, 110, 111, 112, 113, 114, 115.

Coffin, Mary (Mrs. James Coffin, dau. John Severance), 28, 85, 86, 88, 94, 96, 99, 103, 108, 110, 113, 114.

Coffin, Mary (Mrs. Stephen Coffin, dau. George Bunker), 31, 101, 116.

Coffin, Mary (Mrs. Solomon Temple, dau. Thomas Coffin), 98.

Coffin, Miriam (Mrs. Samuel Coffin), 112.

Coffin, Nathaniel, 32, 33, 34, 94.

Coffin, origin of name, 24.

Coffin, Peleg, Esq., 8.

Coffin, Peter, 10, 11, 13, 22, 27, 31, 48.

Coffin, Richard, 24, 85, 95.

Coffin, Ruth (Mrs. William Folger, dau. Richard Coffin), 95.

Coffin, Ruth (Mrs. Richard Coffin), 85, 95.

Coffin, Sally (dau. Thomas Coffin), 97.

Coffin, Samuel, 112.

Coffin School, 33.

Coffin, Stephen, 31, 101, 116.

Coffin, Thomas, 48, 94, 97, 98.

Coffin or Coffyn, Tristram, Sr., 9, 10, 11, 12, 13, 14, 15, 19, 24, 25, 26, 27, 28, 31, 32, 34, 40, 43, 48, 56, 84, 85, 86, 88, 89, 92, 94, 95, 96, 97, 99, 100, 101, 102, 103, 105, 107, 108, 109, 110, 111, 112, 113, 114, 115, 116, 117.

Coffin, Tristram, Jr., 13, 15, 27, 31, 32, 41, 48.

Coffin, William, 34.

Coggeshall Connection with Nantucket, 112.

Coggeshall, Deborah (Mrs. Job Coggeshall), 112, 113.

Coggeshall, Job, 112, 113.

Colcord, Edward, 21.

Coleman, Andrew, 52.

Coleman, Ann (Mrs. Edward Allen, dau. Joseph Coleman), 102.

Coleman, Ann (Mrs. Joseph Coleman), 102.
Coleman, Barnabas, 88.
Coleman, Elihu, 29.
Coleman, Enoch, 52.
Coleman, Hepzibah (Mrs. John Russell, Jr., dau. Barnabas Coleman), 87, 88, 89.
Coleman, Isaac, 19.
Coleman, Jeremiah, 52.
Coleman, Joanna (Mrs. John Coleman, Sr.), 52, 88.
Coleman, John, Jr., 88.
Coleman, John, Sr., 52, 88.
Coleman, Joseph, 102.
Coleman, Lydia, (Mrs. William Mitchell, dau. Andrew Coleman), 52.
Coleman, Nathaniel, 29.
Coleman, Phebe (Mrs. Barzillai Folger), 50.
Coleman, Priscilla (Mrs. John Coleman, Jr.), 88.
Coleman, Rachel (Mrs. Barnabas Coleman), 88.
Coleman, Susanna (Mrs. Thomas Coleman), 102.
Coleman, Thomas, 13, 15, 44, 88, 89, 102, 103.
Collier, Elizabeth (Mrs. Constant Southworth, dau. William Collier), 52.
Collier, Mary (Mrs. Thomas Prence, dau. William Collier), 52, 91.
Collier, Rebecca (dau. William Collier), 52.
Collier, Sarah (Mrs. Love Brewster, dau. William Collier), 52.
Collier, William, 52, 53, 91, 92, 94, 115.
Cope, Caroline, R. (Mrs. Edward Yarnall, dau. Thomas Pim Cope), 97.
Cope, Mary (Mrs. Thomas Pim Cope), 97.
Cope, Thomas Pim, 97.
Cornell, Ezra, 45.
Cutts, John, 37.

Dahlgren, Captain Charles Bunker, 109.
Davis Family, 49.
Deed of Purchase, 11.
Dole, Sarah (Mrs. Edward Greenleaf), 40, 43.
Dongan, Thomas, Governor, 31.
Drinker, Henry, 97.
Drinker, John, 97.

Drinker, Joseph, 97.
Drinker, Mary (Mrs. Henry Drinker), 97.
Drinker, Mary (Mrs. Joseph Drinker), 97.
Drinker, Mary (Mrs. Thomas Pim Cope, dau. John Drinker), 97.
Drinker, Rachel (Mrs. John Drinker), 97.
Drinker, Ruth (Mrs. John Drinker, dau. Benjamin Balch), 97.
Dyer, Mary, 67.

Earle Family, 98, 100.
Earle, John Milton, 98, 99.
Earle, Mary (Mrs. Thomas Earle), 99, 100.
Earle, Sarah (Mrs. John Milton Earle), 99.
Earle, Thomas, 98, 99, 100.
Endicot, John, Esq., 63.
Eric (Earl of Norway), 7.

Farnum Family, 93.
Farrar, Eliza (Mrs. Professor Farrar), 106.
Farrar Family, 93.
Farrar, Professor, 106.
Fforrett, James, 11.
Folger, Abiah (Mrs. Josiah Franklin), 49.
Folger, Abishai, 90, 92, 95.
Folger, Ann (Mrs. James Mitchell, dau. Jethro Folger), 114.
Folger, Anna (Mrs. Thomas Coffin, dau. William Folger), 94, 95, 97, 99.
Folger, Barzillai, 50.
Folger, Benjamin Franklin, 9.
Folger, Bethiah (Mrs. John Barnard, dau. Peter Folger), 45.
Folger, Bethiah (Mrs. Samuel Barker, dau. John Folger), 52, 90.
Folger, Charles James, 54.
Folger, Dorcas (Mrs. Joseph Pratt, dau. Peter Folger), 84, 85.
Folger or Foulger, Eleazor, 14, 15, 49, 50, 95.
Folger, Eleazer, Jr., 49.
Folger, Elizabeth (Mrs. Walter Folger, dau. Thomas Starbuck), 50.
Folger, Experience (Mrs. John Swain, 2d, dau. Peter Folger), 93.
Folger Family, 47, 49.
Folger, Mr. George Howland, 34.
Folger, Jethro, 114.
Folger, Joanna (Mrs. John Coleman, Sr., dau. Peter Folger), 52, 88.

Folger, John, 47, 52, 90, 114.

Folger, Mary (Mrs. Peter Folger), 49, 85, 88, 90, 95.

Folger, Mary (Mrs. Jethro Folger, dau. Nathaniel Starbuck, Jr.), 114.

Folger, Mary (Mrs. John Folger), 90, 114.

Folger, Nathan, 50, 95.

Folger or Foulger, Peter, 9, 13, 14, 45, 47, 48, 49, 50, 51, 52, 54, 68, 85, 86, 87, 88, 89, 90, 92, 93, 94, 95, 97, 100, 114, 115.

Folger, Phebe (Mrs. Barzillai Folger), 50.

Folger, Phebe (Mrs. Uriel Hussey), 98, 99.

Folger, Ruth (Mrs. William Folger), 95.

Folger, Sarah (Mrs. Abishai Folger), 90, 92, 95, 96.

Folger, Sarah (Mrs. Eleazer Folger), 50, 95.

Folger, Sarah (Mrs. Nathan Folger), 95.

Folger, Sarah (Mrs. Tristram Hussey), 98, 99.

Folger, Walter, Jr., 50, 51.

Folger, Walter, Sr., 50.

Folger, William C., 50, 95.

Franciscus, Mr. Albert H., 104.

Franciscus, Susan (Mrs. Albert H. Franciscus, dau. Dr. Paul Swift), 104.

Franklin, Abiah (Mrs. Josiah Franklin, dau. Peter Folger), 49.

Franklin, Benjamin, 47, 49.

Franklin, Deborah Read (Mrs. Benjamin Franklin), 49.

Franklin, Josiah, 49.

Franklin, Sarah (Mrs. Richard Bache, dau. Benjamin Franklin), 49.

Furber, William, 21.

Gardiner, Lion, 55.

Gardiner, Sarah (Mrs. Benjamin Balch), 98.

Gardiner, Thomas, Governor, 55, 60, 85, 86, 88, 89, 91, 92, 94, 95, 96, 97, 98, 100, 102, 103, 105, 107, 108, 109, 113, 116, 117.

Gardner, Anna (Mrs. Solomon Gardner), 100, 116.

Gardner, Deborah (Mrs. John Macy, Sr., dau. Richard Gardner), 20, 84, 85, 87, 88, 94, 95, 105, 116.

Gardner, Dinah (Mrs. David Macy, dau. Solomon Gardner), 116.

Gardner, Dorcas (Mrs. Dr. Paul Swift, dau. Zenas Gardner), 100, 103, 104.

Gardner, Elizabeth (Mrs. Stephen Gorham, dau. James Gardner), 101, 102, 108.

Gardner, Hezikiah, 90, 92.

Gardner, Hope (Mrs. John Coffin, Esq., dau. Richard Gardner), 85, 95, 96.

Gardner, James, 102, 108.

Gardner, John, 55, 56, 57, 58, 89, 91, 92, 94.

Gardner, Mary, 77.

Gardner, Mary (Mrs. James Gardner), 102, 108.

Gardner, Mary (Mrs. Richard Gardner, 2d), 100, 113, 116.

Gardner, Miriam (Mrs. Samuel Coffin, dau. Richard Gardner), 112, 113.

Gardner, Paul, 100.

Gardner, Priscilla (Mrs. Captain John Gardner), 89, 91.

Gardner, Rachel (Mrs. John Brown, Jr., dau. John Gardner), 58, 89, 91.

Gardner, Rachel (Mrs. Paul Gardner), 100.

Gardner, Richard, Sr., 15, 20, 55, 56, 60, 85, 86, 88, 89, 92, 95, 96, 97, 100, 102, 103, 105, 107, 108, 109, 113, 116, 117.

Gardner, Richard, 2d, 100, 113, 116.

Gardner, Sarah (Mrs. Eleazer Folger), 50, 95, 96.

Gardner, Sarah (Mrs. Richard Gardner, Sr.), 20, 55, 60, 85, 88, 95, 96, 100, 102, 105, 108, 113, 116.

Gardner, Sarah (Mrs. Robert Barker, widow Hezikiah Gardner, dau. Abishai Folger), 52, 90, 92.

Gardner, Solomon, 100, 116.

Gardner, Susanna (Mrs. Zenas Gardner), 100.

Gardner, Zenas, 100.

Garrison, William Lloyd, 32.

Gayer, Damaris (Mrs. Nathaniel Coffin), 94, 95.

Gayer, Dorcas (Mrs. Jethro Starbuck, dau. William Gayer), 84, 101, 102, 105, 106.

Gayer, Dorcas (Mrs. William Gayer, dau. Edward Starbuck), 84, 95, 102, 106.

Gayer, William, 84, 95, 102, 106.

Gibbons Family, 100.

Giles, Sarah (Mrs. Zaccheus Macy, 2d, dau. Giles E. Stanton), 117.

Gillespie, Mrs. E. D., 49.

Godfrey, Jane (Mrs. George Bunker), 31.

Goldsmith, Ralph, 64, 65.

Gorges, Sir Fernando or Ferdinand, 9.

Gorham, Desire (Mrs. Zacariah Bunker, dau. Shubael Gorham), 107, 108.

Gorham, Eliza, 29.

Gorham, Elizabeth (Mrs. Stephen Gorham), 101, 108.

Gorham, Puella (Mrs. Shubael Gorham), 108.

Gorham, Shubael, 108.

Gorham, Stephen, 101, 108.

Gorham, Susanna (Mrs. Daniel Paddack, dau. Stephen Gorham), 101, 108.

Gosnold, Biography, 8.

Gottier, Mary (Mrs. Henry Drinker), 97.

Grafton, Priscilla (Mrs. Captain John Gardner), 89, 91.

Grasse, Comte de, 34.

Gray, Alice, (Mrs. Sylvanus Hussey, Jr.), 110.

Greenleaf, Edmund, 27, 28, 40, 43.

Greenleaf, Elizabeth (Mrs. Stephen Greenleaf, dau. Tristram Coffin), 28, 31, 40, 43.

Greenleaf Family, 40.

Greenleaf, Hester (Mrs. Stephen Greenleaf, dau. Nathaniel Weare), 46.

Greenleaf, Margaret (Mrs. Tristram Greenleaf), 43.

Greenleaf, Nathaniel, 43.

Greenleaf, Sarah (Mrs. Edmund Greenleaf), 27, 40, 43.

Greenleaf, Sarah (Mrs. Joseph Whittier, dau. Nathaniel Greenleaf), 43.

Greenleaf, Stephen, Lieutenant, 10, 11, 13, 28, 40, 41, 42, 43, 46, 48.

Greenleaf, Tristram, 43.

Greenly, Elizabeth Brown (Mrs. Sir Isaac Coffin, dau. T. Greenly, Esq.), 35.

Greenly, T., Esq., 35.

Ham, John, 22.

Harvey, Joanna (Mrs. Robert Barnard), 45, 91, 115.

Hathaway Family, 110.

Hathaway, Hepzibah (Mrs. Thomas Hathaway, dau. Nathaniel Starbuck), 111, 112.

Hathaway, Hepzibah (Mrs. Samuel Wing, dau. Thomas Hathaway), 111.

Hathaway, Thomas, 111, 112.

Hazzard, Anna (Mrs. Thomas Hazzard), 106.

Hazzard, Elizabeth, 106.

Hazzard Family, 92.

Hazzard, Thomas, 106.

Herioff (Navigator), 7.

Hobart, Abigail (dau. Rev. Peter Hobart, unmarried), 59.

Hobart, Bathsheba (Mrs. Joseph Turner, dau. Rev. Peter Hobart), 59.

Hobart, David, 59.

Hobart, Edmund, 59, 89, 91, 92, 94.

Hobart, Edmund, 2d, 59.

Hobart, Elizabeth (Mrs. John Ripley, dau. Rev. Peter Hobart), 59.

Hobart or Hubberd Family, 58.

Hobart, Gershom, 59.

Hobart, Hannah, 1st (died soon), 59.

Hobart, Hannah (Mrs. John Brown, of Salem, dau. Rev. Peter Hobart), 58, 59, 89, 91.

Hobart, Icabod, 59.

Hobart, Israel, 59.

Hobart, Jael (Mrs. Joseph Bradford, dau. Rev. Peter Hobart), 59.

Hobart, Japhet, 59.

Hobart, Jeremiah, 59.

Hobart, Joanna (Mrs. David Hobart, dau. Edmund Quincy), 59.

Hobart, Joshua (son of Edmund Hobart), 59.

Hobart, Joshua (son of Rev. Peter Hobart), 59.

Hobart, Josiah, 59.

Hobart, Lydia (Mrs. Captain Thomas Lincoln), 59.

Hobart, Nehemiah, 59.

Hobart, Rebecca, 59.

Hobart, Rebecca (Mrs. Daniel Mason, dau. Rev. Peter Hobart), 59.

Hobart, Rebecca (Mrs. Rev. Peter Hobart), 59.

Hobart or Hubberd, Rev. Peter, 58, 59, 89, 91, 92, 94.

Hobart, Sarah (Mrs. David Hobart), 59.

Hobart, Sarah (dau. Edmund Hobart), 59.

Hobart, Sarah (Mrs. Gershom Hobart), 59.

Hobart, Sarah (Mrs. Israel Hobart, dau. Rev. William Wetherill), 59.

Hobart, Sarah (Mrs. Nehemiah Hobart), 59.
Hobart, Thomas, 59.
Hodge Family, 49.
Holder, Christopher, 60, 115.
Holder, Mary (Mrs. Peleg Slocum), 115.
Hopcot, Sarah (Mrs. Thomas Macy), 20, 84, 85, 87, 93, 94, 96, 105, 108, 116.
Hopkins Family, 92.
Howland, John, 104, 109.
Humphrey Family, 49.
Hussey, Abial (Mrs. Sylvanus Hussey), 88.
Hussey, Abigail (dau. Stephen Hussey), 39.
Hussey, Alice (Mrs. Sylvanus Hussey, Jr.), 110.
Hussey, Batchelder or Bachiler, 39, 98.
Hussey, Christopher, 10, 11, 13, 37, 38, 43, 44, 86, 88, 89, 99, 101, 103, 108, 109, 110, 111.
Hussey, Daniel, 39.
Hussey, Deborah (Mrs. George Hussey), 98, 101.
Hussey, George, 39, 98, 101.
Hussey, Hepzibah (Mrs. Sylvanus Hussey, Sr.), 98, 101, 110.
Hussey, Hulda (Mrs. John Smith), 38.
Hussey, John, 37, 38.
Hussey, Joseph, 38.
Hussey, Lydia (Mrs. Sylvanus Hussey, Jr.), 110, 111.
Hussey, Martha (Mrs. Stephen Hussey), 38, 88, 98, 101, 108, 110.
Hussey, Mary (dau. Christopher Hussey), 38.
Hussey, Mary (Mrs. John Hussey), 37.
Hussey, Mary (Mrs. Thomas Earle, dau. Uriel Hussey), 99, 100.
Hussey, Phebe (Mrs. Uriel Hussey), 98.
Hussey, Puella (Mrs. Shubael Gorham, dau. Stephen Hussey), 39, 108.
Hussey, Rachel (Mrs. Barnabas Coleman, dau. Sylvanus Hussey), 88.
Hussey, Rebecca (Mrs. John Hussey), 38.
Hussey, Robert, 43.
Hussey, Sarah (Mrs. Tristram Hussey), 98.
Hussey, Sarah (Mrs. John Milton Earle, dau. Tristram Hussey), 99.

Hussey, Stephen, 38, 39, 78, 88, 98, 99, 101, 103, 108, 109, 110, 111.
Hussey, Susanna (Mrs. Zenas Gardner, dau. George Hussey), 100, 101.
Hussey, Sylvanus, Jr., 110.
Hussey, Sylvanus, Sr., 39, 88, 98, 101, 110, 111.
Hussey, Theodata (Mrs. Christopher Hussey, dau. Rev. Stephen Batchilder), 37, 38, 88, 99, 101, 108, 110.
Hussey, Theodata (dau. Christopher Hussey), 38.
Hussey, Theodata (dau. Stephen Hussey), 39.
Hussey, Tristram, 98, 99.
Hussey, Uriel, 98, 99.

Ibrook, Richard, 59.
Indian Deed, 13.
Irwin Family, 49.

Jackson, Sarah (Mrs. Nehemiah Hobart), 59.
James, Duke of York, 57, 58.
Janney, Mary (Mrs. Joseph Drinker), 97.
Johnson, Hannah (Mrs. Paul Wing Newhall), 111, 112.
Joyce, Sarah (Mrs. David Hobart, second wife), 59.

Kinsey, John, 76.
Kirkbride Family, 93.
Knight, Sir Georges, 11.

Lamson, Edwin, 104.
Lamson, Mary (Mrs. Edwin Lamson, dau. Dr. Paul Swift), 104.
Lea & Bunker, 109.
Le Clerc (Coffin), 25.
Leddra, W., 64, 67.
Lief (Navigator), 7.
Lincoln, Lydia (Mrs. Thomas Lincoln, dau. Rev. Peter Hobart), 59.
Lincoln, Thomas, Captain, 59.
Long, Robert, 41.
Look, Thomas, 15.
Lovelace, Francis, Governor, 16, 26, 27, 55, 57, 59.

Macy, Abigail (Mrs. Benjamin Stanton, dau. David Macy), 116, 117.
Macy, David, 116.
Macy, Deborah (Mrs. Benjamin Coffin), 94.
Macy, Deborah (Mrs. Daniel Russell, dau. John Macy), 87.

Macy, Deborah (Mrs. John Macy, Sr.), 20, 84, 87, 94, 105, 116.
Macy, Deborah (Mrs. Thomas Macy³), 84, 94, 105.
Macy, Dinah (Mrs. David Macy), 116.
Macy, Francis, 84.
Macy, George, 20.
Macy, John, Jr., 116.
Macy, John, Sr., 20, 84, 87, 94, 105, 116.
Macy, Judith (Mrs. Francis Macy), 84.
Macy, Judith (Mrs. John Macy, Jr.), 116.
Macy, Love (Mrs. James Cartwright, dau. Francis Macy), 84.
Macy, Love (Mrs. Joseph Rotch, dau. Thomas Macy³), 104, 105.
Macy, Mary (Mrs. William Bunker, dau. Thomas Macy), 85, 93, 96, 103, 108, 109.
Macy, Paul, 113.
Macy, Samuel, 20.
Macy, Sarah (Mrs. Thomas Macy), 20, 84, 85, 87, 93, 94, 96, 105, 108, 116.
Macy, Sarah (Mrs. Zaccheus Macy, 2d, dau. Giles E. Stanton), 117.
Macy, signification of name, 20.
Macy, Thomas, 9, 10, 11, 12, 13, 17, 19, 20, 22, 26, 44, 48, 84, 85, 86, 87, 89, 92, 93, 94, 96, 97, 100, 103, 105, 107, 108, 109, 113, 116, 117.
Macy, Thomas³, 94, 105.
Macy, Zaccheus, 1st, 117.
Macy, Zaccheus, 2d, 117.
Mason, Daniel, 59.
Mason, Rebecca (Mrs. Daniel Mason, dau. Rev. Peter Hobart), 59.
Mather, Cotton, 48, 57.
Mayhew, Experience, 71.
Mayhew Family, 68.
Mayhew, Jane (Mrs. Thomas Mayhew, Jr.), 96.
Mayhew, John, 70, 71.
Mayhew, Jonathan, 71.
Mayhew, Mary (Mrs. Paine Mayhew), 96.
Mayhew, Matthew, 70, 96.
Mayhew, Paine, 96.
Mayhew, Sarah (Mrs. Abishai Folger), 90, 92, 95, 96.
Mayhew, Simon, 68.
Mayhew, Thomas, Sr., 9, 10, 11, 12, 13, 48, 68, 69, 70, 92, 96, 97, 100.

Mayhew, Thomas, Jr., 15, 47, 68, 69, 70, 92, 96, 97, 100.
Mayhew, Thomas, 3d, 70, 71.
Mellor Family, 93.
Mitchell, Ann (Mrs. James Mitchell), 114.
Mitchell, Elizabeth (Mrs. Richard Mitchell, Jr.), 83, 115.
Mitchell Family, 83.
Mitchell, Hepzibah (Mrs. David Buffum, 1st, dau. James Mitchell), 114, 115.
Mitchell, James, 114, 115.
Mitchell, Lydia (Mrs. Peleg Mitchell, Sr.), 83, 86, 87.
Mitchell, Lydia (Mrs. William Mitchell), 51.
Mitchell, Love (Mrs. Judge Brayton), 86.
Mitchell, Maria, 51, 87.
Mitchell, Mary (Mrs. Richard Mitchell, Sr.), 83.
Mitchell, Mary (Mrs. Richard Mitchell, 3d), 83.
Mitchell, Peleg, Sr., 83, 86, 87.
Mitchell, Richard, Jr., 83, 115.
Mitchell, Richard, Sr., 83.
Mitchell, Richard, 3d, 83.
Mitchell, William, 51.
Mitchells, Nantucket, 115.
Montague, John, 34.
Moore, Katharine (Mrs. Marcus A. Moore), 104.
Moore, Marcus A., 104.
Morrell, Mary (Mrs. Peter Folger), 85, 88, 90, 95.
Morris, Wil., 64.
Morse, Benjamin, 32.
Morse, Margaret (Mrs. Joseph Coffin, dau. Benjamin Morse), 32.
Mott Family, 92, 94, 99.
Mott, James, 97.
Mott, Lucretia (Mrs. James Mott), 97, 99.

Newhall, Estes, 111.
Newhall Family, 93.
Newhall, Hannah (Mrs. Paul Wing Newhall), 111, 112.
Newhall, Hepzibah (Mrs. Estes Newhall, dau. Paul and Abigail Wing), 111.
Newhall, Paul Wing, 111, 112.
Nicolls, Mathias, 57.
Norman, Lucy (Mrs. David Stanton), 116.
Noyes, Nicolas, 41.
Noyes, Thomas, 41.

Paddack, Ann (Mrs. Nathaniel Paddack, dau. William Bunker), 93, 103, 108.

Paddack, Daniel, 101, 103, 108.

Paddack, Deborah (Mrs. George Hussey, dau. Daniel Paddack), 98, 101.

Paddack, Deborah (Mrs. Zechariah Paddack), 98.

Paddack, Lydia (Mrs. Shubael Bunker, dau. Daniel Paddack), 107, 108.

Paddack, Mary (Mrs. Francis Swain, Sr., dau. Nathaniel Paddack), 93.

Paddack, Nathaniel, 93, 103, 108.

Paddack, Susanna (Mrs. Daniel Paddack), 101, 108.

Paddack, Zechariah, 98.

Paine, Jane (Mrs. Thomas Mayhew, Jr.), 96.

Pelham, Martha (Mrs. Peter Pelham, dau. Thomas Coffin), 98.

Pelham, Peter, 98.

Pepper Family, 49.

Perkins, Mary (Mrs. Lieutenant Isaac Chase), 91.

Perry, Commodore, 49.

Perry Family, 49.

Pickard, S. T., 43.

Pierce, Daniel, 41.

Pierce, David, 41.

Phelps, Nicholas, 62.

Phillips, Elizabeth (Mrs. John E. Phillips, dau. Dr. Paul Swift), 104.

Phillips, Mr. John E., 104.

Pike or Pyke Family, 44.

Pike, Robert, 13, 15, 19, 44.

Pike, William, 10, 11.

Pile, William, 48.

Pinkham, Hebsibeth (Mrs. Nathan Bunker[1]), 107.

Piper, Margaret (Mrs. Tristram Greenleaf), 43.

Pratt, Bethiah (Mrs. Sampson Cartwright, dau. Joseph Pratt), 84.

Pratt, Dorcas (Mrs. Joseph Pratt), 84.

Pratt, Joseph, 84.

Prence, Judith (Mrs. Isaac Barker, dau. Thomas Prence), 52, 90, 91.

Prence, Mary (Mrs. Thomas Prence, dau. William Collier), 52, 91.

Prence, Thomas, Governor, 52, 53, 54, 91, 92, 94, 115.

Proprietors, Associates, 15.

Proprietors, Nine original, 10.

Quincy, Edmund, 59.

Quincy, Joanna (Mrs. David Hobart, dau. Edmund Quincy), 59.

Rankin, Mary (Mrs. Paine Mayhew), 96.

Rawson, Edward, 66.

Read, Deborah (Mrs. Benjamin Franklin), 49.

Read, Sarah (Mrs. Richard Bache, dau. Benjamin Franklin), 49.

Reynear, Rachel (Mrs. John Drinker), 97.

Reynolds, Katharine (Mrs. Edward Starbuck), 21, 27, 28, 84, 86, 87, 88, 95, 99, 101, 102, 103, 105, 106, 109, 112, 113, 114, 117.

Richardson, John, 72, 115.

Ripley, Elizabeth (Mrs. John Ripley, dau. Peter Hobart), 59.

Ripley, John, 59.

Robinson, William, 17, 67.

Rodman, Anna, 106.

Rodman, Samuel, 106.

Rolfe, John, 48.

Rotch, Benjamin, 106.

Rotch, Eliza (dau. Benjamin Rotch), 100, 107.

Rotch, Elizabeth (Mrs. William Rotch), 104, 106.

Rotch Family, 93, 104.

Rotch, Joseph, 104, 106.

Rotch, Love (Mrs. Joseph Rotch), 104.

Rotch, Mary, 106.

Rotch, William, 104, 106, 107.

Russell, Daniel, 87.

Russell, Deborah (Mrs. Daniel Russell), 87.

Russell Family, 87.

Russell, Hepzibah (Mrs. John Russell, Jr.), 87, 89.

Russell, John, Jr., 87, 89.

Russell, John, Sr., 87.

Russell, Ruth (Mrs. John Russell, Sr.), 87.

Salter, William, 66.

Sanborn, John, 38.

Sanborn, Stephen, 38.

Sanborn, William, 38.

Schönberg, Baron, 93.

Searle, Edward, 12.

Sears, Deborah (Mrs. Zechariah Paddack, dau. Richard Sears), 98.

Sears, Dorothy (Mrs. Richard Sears), 98.

Sears, Richard, 98.

Severance, Abigail (Mrs. John Severance), 28.

Severance, John, 28.

Severance, Mary (Mrs. James Coffin, dau. John Severance), 28, 85, 86, 88, 94, 96, 99, 103, 108, 110, 113, 114.

Shattuck, Damaris, 60.

Shattuck Family, 60.

Shattuck, Retire, 66.

Shattuck, Return, 66.

Shattuck, Samuel, 60, 62, 64, 65, 66, 67.

Shattuck, Sarah (Mrs. Richard Gardner, Sr., dau. Samuel Shattuck), 20, 55, 60, 85, 88, 95, 96, 100, 102, 105, 108, 113, 116.

Sherburne (original name of Nantucket), 15.

Sibley, Mark H., 54.

Sigourney Family, 93.

Slocum, Elizabeth, 115.

Slocum, Mary (Mrs. Peleg Slocum), 115.

Slocum, Peleg, 72, 75, 77, 115.

Smith, Deborah (Mrs. Nathaniel Batchilder), 39.

Smith or Smyth, Edward, 22.

Smith, Hulda (Mrs. John Smith, dau. Christopher Hussey), 38.

Smith, John, 12, 13, 15, 38, 48.

Somerby, Henry, 27.

Somerby, Judith (Mrs. Tristram Coffin, Jr., widow Henry Somerby, dau. Edmund Greenleaf), 27.

Southwick, Cassandra, 62, 63.

Southwick, Josiah, 62.

Southwick, Lawrence, 62, 63.

Southworth, Constant, 52.

Southworth, Elizabeth (Mrs. Constant Southworth, dau. William Collier), 52.

Stanton, Abigail (Mrs. Benjamin Stanton, dau. David Macy), 117.

Stanton, Benjamin, 116, 117.

Stanton Connection, 116.

Stanton, David, 116.

Stanton, Edwin Macy, 116, 117.

Stanton, Giles E., 117.

Stanton, Hannah (Mrs. Giles E. Stanton), 117.

Stanton, Lucy (Mrs. David Stanton), 116.

Starbuck, Abigail (Mrs. Peter Coffin, dau. Edward Starbuck), 22, 27.

Starbuck, Deborah (Mrs. Tristram Starbuck), 112.

Starbuck, Deborah (Mrs. Job Coggeshall, dau. Tristram Starbuck), 112, 113.

Starbuck, Dinah (Mrs. Nathaniel Starbuck, Jr., dau. James Coffin), 87, 99, 102, 110, 112, 114.

Starbuck, Dorcas (Mrs. William Gayer, dau. Edward Starbuck), 14, 84, 95, 102, 106.

Starbuck, Dorcas (Mrs. Jethro Starbuck), 84, 101, 105.

Starbuck, Edward, 9, 13, 14, 15, 19, 21, 22, 23, 27, 28, 48, 84, 86, 87, 88, 89, 95, 97, 99, 101, 102, 103, 105, 106, 107, 109, 110, 111, 112, 113, 114, 115, 117.

Starbuck, Elizabeth (Mrs. Walter Folger, dau. Thomas Starbuck), 50.

Starbuck, Elizabeth (Mrs. Stephen Greenleaf, dau. Tristram Coffin, Sr.), 28, 31, 40, 43.

Starbuck, Hepzibah (Mrs. Sylvanus Hussey, Sr., dau. Nathaniel Starbuck, Jr.), 98, 99, 101, 102, 110.

Starbuck, Hepzibah (Mrs. Thomas Hathaway, dau. Nathaniel Starbuck, Sr.), 111.

Starbuck, Jethro, 30, 84, 101, 105.

Starbuck, Katharine (Mrs. Edward Starbuck), 21, 27, 28, 84, 86, 87, 88, 95, 99, 101, 102, 103, 105, 106, 109, 110, 111, 112, 113, 114, 117.

Starbuck, Lydia (Mrs. Benjamin Barney, dau. Jethro Starbuck), 105.

Starbuck, Mary (Mrs. James Gardner, dau. Nathaniel Starbuck, Sr.), 102, 103, 108, 109.

Starbuck, Mary (Mrs. Jethro Folger, dau. Nathaniel Starbuck, Jr.), 114.

Starbuck, Mary (Mrs. Nathaniel Starbuck, Sr., dau. Tristram Coffin, Sr.), 23, 28, 29, 30, 31, 72, 75, 76, 77, 78, 84, 87, 88, 99, 101, 102, 103, 105, 109, 110, 111, 112, 114, 115.

Starbuck, Mary (Mrs. Richard Mitchell, 3d, dau. Jethro Starbuck), 83, 84.

Starbuck, Mary (dau. Nathaniel Starbuck, Sr.), 103.

Starbuck, Nathaniel, Jr., 72, 75, 77, 87, 99, 102, 110, 112, 114.

Starbuck, Nathaniel, Sr., 15, 23, 28, 29, 30, 48, 75, 77, 84, 87, 88, 99, 101, 102, 103, 105, 109, 110, 111, 112, 114.

Starbuck, Priscilla (Mrs. John Coleman, Jr., dau. Nathaniel Starbuck), 88.

Starbuck, Rachel (Mrs. Paul Gardner, dau. Thomas Starbuck), 100, 101.

Starbuck, Rachel (Mrs. Thomas Starbuck), 101.

Starbuck, Ruth (Mrs. John Russell, Sr., dau. Nathaniel Starbuck, Jr.), 87.

Starbuck, Sarah (Mrs. Joseph Austin, dau. Edward Starbuck), 22, 30, 86, 95, 101, 105, 113, 117.

Starbuck, signification of name, 23.

Starbuck, Thomas, 50, 101.

Starbuck, Tristram, 112.

Stephenson, Marmaduke, 17, 67.

Stevens, Dionis (Mrs. Tristram Coffin, Sr., dau. Robert Stevens), 24, 40, 43, 84, 85, 88, 89, 94, 95, 96, 97, 99, 101, 102, 103, 105, 108, 109, 110, 111, 112, 113, 114, 115, 116.

Stevens, Robert, 24.

Steward, Eben, 29.

Story, Thomas, 72, 75, 115.

Swain, Elizabeth (Mrs. Nathaniel Swain), 46.

Swain, Elizabeth (Mrs. Nathaniel Weare, dau. Richard Swain), 45, 46.

Swain, Elizabeth (Mrs. Richard Swain), 93.

Swain, Experience (Mrs. John Swain, 2d), 93.

Swain Family, 93.

Swain, Francis, Jr., 93.

Swain, Francis, Sr., 93.

Swain, Jane (Mrs. Richard Swain, widow George Bunker), 45, 46.

Swain or Swayne, John, 1st, 10, 11, 13, 45, 46, 48, 78, 93.

Swain, John, 2d, 93.

Swain, John, 3d, 93.

Swain, Lydia (Mrs. Francis Swain, Jr.), 93.

Swain, Mary (Mrs. Francis Swain, Sr.), 93.

Swain, Mary (Mrs. John Swain, 1st, dau. Nathaniel Wyer), 45, 46, 93.

Swain, Mary (Mrs. John Swain, 3d), 93.

Swain or Swayne, Richard, 10, 11, 13, 45, 46, 48, 93.

Swett, Benjamin, 46.

Swett, Hester (Mrs. Benjamin Swett, dau. Nathaniel Weare), 46.

Swett, Mary (Mrs. John Swain, 3d), 93.

Swift, Content (Mrs. Zaccheus Wing), 111.

Swift, Dorcas (Mrs. Dr. Paul Swift), 100, 103, 104.

Swift, Elizabeth (Mrs. John E. Phillips, dau. Dr. Paul Swift), 104.

Swift Family, 100.

Swift, Kathrine (Mrs. (1st) Dr. Marcus A. Moore; Mrs. (2d) Robert Wharton; dau. Dr. Paul Swift), 104.

Swift, Mary (Mrs. Edwin Lamson, dau. Dr. Paul Swift), 104.

Swift, Dr. Paul, 100, 103, 104.

Swift, Susan (Mrs. Albert H. Franciscus, dau. Dr. Paul Swift), 104.

Temple, Mary (Mrs. Solomon Temple), 98.

Temple, Solomon, 98.

Thatcher, Dorothy (Mrs. Richard Sears), 98.

Tilley, John, 104, 109.

Tripp, Elizabeth (Mrs. Richard Mitchell, Jr.), 83, 115.

Turner, Bathsheba (Mrs. Joseph Turner, dau. Peter Hobart), 59.

Turner, Joseph, 59.

Van Leer Family, 100.

Vane, Sir Harry, 44.

Vines, Richard, 11.

Walderne, Richard, 21.

Walter and Janney Families, 113.

Wannackmanack (Indian), 12, 14, 15.

Wannackmanack Receipt, 14.

Ward Family, 93.

Wawinnesit (Indian), 13.

Weare, Weir, Weyer, Wier, Wire, Wyer, 46.

Weare, Elizabeth (Mrs. Nathaniel Weare[2], dau. Richard Swain), 45, 46.

Weare Family, 46.

Weare or Wire, Hester (Mrs. Benjamin Swett), 46.

Weare, Mary (Mrs. John Swain, 1st, dau. Nathaniel Wier), 45, 46, 93.

Weare, Nathaniel, 45, 46.

Weare, Nathaniel, 2d, 46.

Weare, Nathaniel, 3d, 46.

Weare, Peter, 45, 46.

Weare, Robert, 46.

Webster, Daniel, 39.

Wetherill, Sarah (Mrs. Israel Hobart, dau. Rev. William Wetherill), 59.

Wetherill, William, Rev., 59.

Wharton, Edward, 17, 18.

Wharton Family, 93.

Wharton, Katharine (Mrs. Robert Wharton, dau. Dr. Paul Swift), 104.
Wharton, Robert, 104.
White Family, 100.
Whittier, John Greenleaf, 43.
Whittier, Joseph, 2d, 43.
Whittier, Sarah (Mrs. Joseph Whittier, 2d, dau. Nathaniel Greenleaf), 43.
Wiggan, Captain Thomas, 22.
Wiggins, Thomas, 21, 22.
William, Earl of Sterling, 9, 10.
Wing, Abigail (Mrs. Paul Wing), 111.
Wing Connection, 110.
Wing, Content (Mrs. Zaccheus Wing), 111.
Wing, Deborah (Mrs. John Wing, dau. Rev. Stephen Batchilder), 38, 110.
Wing, Hepzibah (Mrs. Estes Newhall, dau. Paul Wing), 111.
Wing, Hepzibah (Mrs. Samuel Wing), 111.
Wing, John, 38, 110.
Wing, Lydia (Mrs. Sylvanus Hussey, Jr., dau. Samuel Wing), 110, 111.

Wing, Paul, 111.
Wing, Samuel, 111.
Wing, Zaccheus, 111.
Winthrop, Governor, 44.
Winthrop, John, Esq., 10.
Wisner, Henry, 112.
Wisner, Henry A., 112.
Wood, Mary (Mrs. John Hussey), 37.
Wood, Mary (Mrs. Richard Mitchell, Sr.), 83.
Woodbridge, Mrs. Mary A., (dau. Judge Brayton), 86.
Worth, Judith (Mrs. John Macy, Jr.), 116.
Worth, Justice of Peace, 30.
Wyer, Mary (see Weare), 46.
Wyer, Robert (see Weare), 46.
Wyman, Mary (Mrs. Nathaniel Batchilder), 39.

Yarnall, Benjamin H., 97.
Yarnall, Caroline R. (Mrs. Edward Yarnall, dau. Thomas Pim Cope), 97.
Yarnall, Edward, 97.
Yarnall, Eliza (Mrs. Benjamin H. Yarnall), 97.

THE END.